T0311527

# The Unstoppable Sales Team

Why are companies like Salesforce, Whirlpool, and Cintas repeatedly recognized for their top sales performance? What are they doing that sets them apart from their competition, allowing them to increase sales revenue year over year? It's not a result of their ability to master online sales funnels or introduce software that automates their sales process. Instead, these companies dominate in their markets because they continually elevate their sales team's performance to the level of being unstoppable.

This book is written for sales executives, sales leaders, and sales managers. If you lead a sales team and want to accelerate their performance without being forced to invest in new technology, hire more employees or completely restructure your existing sales team, then this book is for you.

*The Unstoppable Sales Team* contains the lessons learned, best practices and observations applied through the author's work with sales teams globally. Building on his popular book *The Unstoppable Sales Machine*, the author shares the best strategies for building a high-performing sales team that outsells and outperforms their competition.

# The Unstoppable Sales Team

## Elevate Your Team's Performance, Win More Business, and Attract Top Performers

Shawn Casemore

Routledge
Taylor & Francis Group

A PRODUCTIVITY PRESS BOOK

First published 2024
by Routledge
605 Third Avenue, New York, NY 10158

and by Routledge
4 Park Square, Milton Park, Abingdon, Oxon, OX14 4RN

*Routledge is an imprint of the Taylor & Francis Group, an informa business*

ISBN: 978-1-032-39151-9 (hbk)
ISBN: 978-1-032-39150-2 (pbk)
ISBN: 978-1-003-34861-0 (ebk)

DOI: 10.4324/9781003348610

Typeset in Minion Pro
by KnowledgeWorks Global Ltd.

# Contents

**PART III    A Sales Leader's Guide to
Managing an Unstoppable Sales Team**

# About the Author

**Shawn Casemore** is a professional speaker, consultant, and advisor. He is the Owner and Founder of Casemore and Co Inc., a global consulting firm, and has worked with organizations such as CN Rail, Tim Hortons, Pepsi Co, MNP, Bank of Montreal, and over 200 other leading organizations. In addition, he's served on several boards, including the Canadian Association of Family-Owned Enterprises and Excellence in Manufacturing Consortium.

His speaking typically includes over two dozen keynotes each year at major conferences, and he's lectured at institutions such as the University of Waterloo and Humber Institute of Technology and Advanced Learning.

Shawn's publishing includes hundreds of articles in print and online for publications such as *Forbes, Fast Company, Chief Executive, Industry Week*, and *The Globe and Mail*. He's also written three commercially published books, including his most recent, *The Unstoppable Sales Machine* (Taylor and Francis, 2022).

# Introduction

This book is written for sales executives, sales leaders, and managers. If you lead or manage a sales team and want to improve their ability to sell, individually and collectively as a team, supporting them to reach new levels of performance that are unstoppable, then this book is for you.

It contains the lessons learned and best practices applied through all my work with clients from around the globe. Building on my work with Unstoppable Organizations and helping hundreds of companies introduce what I refer to as Unstoppable Sales Machines, this book captures my clients' best strategies in building high-performing sales teams that repeatedly outsell and outperform their competition.

To provide you with the most current and up-to-date information, a virtual appendix will be available immediately at www.unstoppablesales. team. You can visit this site anytime to obtain updated tools and resources for building your very own *Unstoppable Sales Team*.

My latest thinking, models, and strategies for building an unstoppable sales team are contained here, including the Sales Team Accelerator, Sales Performer Attraction Method, and Unstoppable Sales Team Leadership Guide. I'll also be demonstrating how you can quickly establish your *Unstoppable Sales Team* regardless of the size of your company, the sector, or the level of skill your existing sales team possesses. If you sell business to business and have more than one person in a sales-related position, then you can build your very own *Unstoppable Sales Team*, just as countless others have.

Finally, building your sales team to unstoppable levels will not require that you fire anyone or hire dozens of new high-performing (and high-cost) sales professionals. Instead, many of my clients have been able to upskill and re-invigorate their existing sales team to reach new levels of sales success. This book accepts you where you are and then walks you through the steps to quickly elevate and accelerate your sales team's performance. You'll find all the advice, guidance, case studies, and worksheets contained in this one convenient book ready for you to implement.

If you want to grow or accelerate your sales, you'll need a high-performing sales team to do so. This book will provide you with the insights, tools, and methods to do so.

**Shawn Casemore**
*Chatsworth, ON*
*December 2022*

# Part I

# Why You Need a Strong Sales Team (Not Just Strong Sales Performers)

As I've shared in my book, *The Unstoppable Sales Machine*, selling has changed. Moreover, the people who are deciding to make a career in sales have also changed. For this reason, trying to find a "hunter" or "top performing" sales professional is becoming more and more difficult. Further to this, my studies and work have concluded that the strongest sales teams aren't built on having star performers but rather contain a dynamic group of individuals with a common goal, willing to continuously learn, develop, and grow, all while supporting one other.

With the worry about finding a star performer now out of the way, let's jump in to how to build your unstoppable sales team starting from where you are right now.

DOI: 10.4324/9781003348610-1

# 1

## Start from Where You Are Right Now

The whole is greater than the sum of its parts.

**Aristotle**
*Greek Philosopher*

### ONE THING THAT HASN'T CHANGED ABOUT SELLING

When it comes to growing your sales, many of the executives I meet are under the impression that achieving their revenue targets requires several high-performing sales professionals. While I'll admit that sales superstars can be worth their weight in gold when generating new business, there are other more important considerations.

Suppose you wanted to save money on gas. You could trade in your current vehicle (likely at a loss), buy a new, likely expensive electric car, and immediately cut your fuel costs. But what would be the actual cost of making this shift to avoid paying fuel prices?

- Increased investment: You'd invest anywhere from $15k to $30k more in buying a new electric vehicle, not including a potential loss of value in trading in your existing car.
- Additional costs: If financing, you'd pay the interest on this additional investment; if maintenance is required, it is likely to cost more than on a typical combustion vehicle.

DOI: 10.4324/9781003348610-2

- Inconvenience: If you travel any distance, you'd need to plan ahead to ensure you can sustain a charge in your vehicle.

My point isn't to make an argument for or against electric vehicles or the additional benefits they provide for the environment. Instead, I'm demonstrating that in some instances investing in the latest and greatest can lead to additional costs that aren't fully understood and that, over the long term, can wind up costing you more.

For this reason, in my work with global organizations, I always suggest that a sales team is built by recognizing all the factors that impact sales. For example:

- Are your sales processes effective at generating new business repeatedly?
- Do you use technology that assists (rather than hinders) the productivity and effectiveness of your sales team?
- Are you aligning the priorities between departments such as Marketing, Business Development, and Customer Service?
- Does your sales team have the skills to sell in the current economy?
- Are you measuring performance indicators individualized to each salesperson (I call this the sales math, which we'll discuss later in the book)?
- Do you have a coaching culture where your sales team is proactively coached and rewarded to elevate their performance?

Building an unstoppable sales team requires far more than hiring a few high performers; it requires the proper structure, processes, skills development, and reinforcement mechanisms to ensure you get the most from your sales team.

In the subsequent chapters, we will discuss how to build an unstoppable sales team and continue elevating their performance while motivating them to sell and stay. I'll share examples of companies who use similar approaches to build their sales teams to unstoppable proportions throughout this book.

When I first entered the profession of sales in my mid-twenties, I learned a thing or two about how to build a strong sales team from my sales manager, Bob. A career car salesman, Bob had been in the business for decades and had worked alongside the dealer principal to structure a high-performing sales team. Of course, everyone in the group received the same training, but Bob treated each salesperson as a unique individual. He individualized sales metrics, such as the number of cars to sell each month and used proactive one-to-one coaching to develop his teams skills, rather than retroactive ranting (often found behind closed doors in many car dealerships). For example, after initially struggling to move potential customers from the parking lot to my office to discuss pricing, Bob took time to sit in on some of my prospect discussions and demonstrate a better approach.

It was through Bob that I learned several lessons in leading a sales team that I advise the sales executives and leaders I work with today to apply, namely:

- Hire for fit within the sales team and company culture, rather than strictly based on a sales track record.
- Focus your efforts and time on building up your team rather than constantly looking for better talent.
- Individualize both training and coaching to the person. Not everyone absorbs training lessons and information at the same speed or manner.
- Set individualized goals based on where the salesperson is and what they could achieve.
- Always encourage reviewing past training materials or lessons rather than constantly introducing new ideas or materials. Allow your team to get the fundamentals down before introducing new ideas or concepts.

For a moment then, let's address the elephant in the room. Do you actually need some top sales performers to round out your team? Possibly, but before you invest the time and money to find one, keep reading.

## WHAT YOU NEED ISN'T WHAT YOU THINK

While recently looking at some old photos of my parents, I came across one that showed my mother in a small metal tub on my grandparent's porch. She seemed happy sitting in the tub, even though, as the oldest of six, she was often the last to get bathed; hence, the water was well-used water by the time she jumped in. Growing up in the 1940s, her parents knew that you didn't need fresh water to bathe your child if you added some warm water to it.

I'll admit that sharing bathwater might seem a bit far-fetched in today's day and age, but there's an important lesson here. We can often achieve our desired outcomes, in this case, a clean child, without starting anew.

Pick up any sales book today and you'll most likely find recommendations to introduce something new. But, of course, this "something" is often what the author or their company specializes in or sells.

A new approach for selling to challenging buyers.
New technology that will revolutionize how you sell.
A new (and simple) sales system.

There are several vital issues these suggestions of "new" tend to miss:

1. They don't focus on the sales team but rather the "new" solution.
2. They fail to consider the skills and experience of your sales team at present.
3. They don't accommodate your industry, customers, or market.
4. They can cost a lot in terms of money and time.
5. They can be frustrating for your sales team to endure.

Most fail to address the most crucial component of your sales team… the team itself. If improving and accelerating your sales required a simple change in process or technology, everyone would have done it by now. I would guess that as you read this, you may yourself have completed some sales training or added a new CRM (Customer Relationship Management) software, and yet you still aren't seeing the results you expect or need.

Instead place your efforts and focus and concentrate on your sales team. After all your team decides the extent to which they apply sales training, the extent to which they use your existing sales processes, what improvements or adjustments they make, and the extent to which they adopt and use your CRM.

In my experience, working with sales teams of Fortune 500 and Fortune 1000 companies globally, there are common truths that have always been the case with sales professionals, which reinforce why hiring new talent isn't always the best approach.

Here are three common truths of today's sales professionals:

1. It has always been challenging to find good sales talent.
   When I was young, those who entered the sales profession were typically unskilled and enjoyed working with people. They were often misfits who had tried other careers and enjoyed some of the freedoms and compensation they could achieve working in sales. Today's sales professionals usually arrive with university degrees and are more intentional (and therefore more prepared) to enter a career in sales. As a result, fewer professionals may be in the market, but those who are come highly educated.

2. Strong sales performers always seek their next opportunity.
   In my mid-twenties, I had my first real experience in sales when I began selling cars. I had the great fortune of working alongside Dan, who had previously worked in a purchasing role and had decided to "move to the other side of the desk," so to speak. His good-natured personality, coupled with his ability to build strong relationships, never rushing the sale, meant that customers continuously came back to buy from him. After about 10 years into his role, Dan decided he needed a new challenge and promptly sought out and was quickly hired as assistant sales manager at a different dealership. The lesson here, good sales talent always seeks to advance their career, challenges, and income.

3. Strong sales performers are intrapreneurs.
   If you've ever owned or run a business, you'll know that it takes a particular person to maintain the drive and motivation to keep pressing ahead, despite the many challenges encountered as an entrepreneur. In many cases, the freedom and ability to set your schedule and choose your income (which are all reliant on how hard one works) is a motivating factor behind being an entrepreneur. Strong sales performers are no different. They seek the ability to manage their time, schedule, and income levels. When any of these factors are impacted or restricted by their boss, company policies or culture, they tend to start looking elsewhere for new opportunities.

For this reason, we need to work to ensure our strong sales performers have the independence they seek. Through the hundreds of sales teams, I work with each year, I can tell you that this is still a driving force behind entering the sales profession today.

My point is simple. We are better off engaging with and building upon the skills and talent we already have today rather than recruiting a top sales performer (or several top performers) to join our team. Your existing team, although they may not be setting the world on fire, have tenure to ensure any investment in their abilities provides a significant and lasting return for your company, for example:

- They've proven they are somewhat content in our existing culture.
- The role expectations and compensation satisfy their current needs.
- They have a good understanding of how we operate as a business.
- We have already made a significant investment in their onboarding and development.
- They have an existing client or customer base.
- Presumably, they have a good grasp on our market and products or services.
- We've already achieved a return on our hiring and onboarding investment.
- They would be appreciative of more income.

The good news then is that you already have a great foundation to build your unstoppable sales team. Additionally you avoid worries about losing a new star performer whom you've invested a fortune to attract and hire. Nevertheless, there will be some points along your team-building journey where hiring will make sense.

### STORIES FROM THE SALES FLOOR

While working with a manufacturer of the equipment, the Vice President of Sales asked me what new systems would help his team sell more.

He mentioned some of the more common CRM software brands and asked about my experience with them and if I had any recommendations.

"What you have right now is fine," I responded. He seemed a bit dumbfounded, so I continued.

"They already have simple methods in place to track their leads and progress with each, so a new CRM at this point would only serve to create a distraction from selling. Instead, let's get some simple tools into their hands to enable them apply some of the skills we've been working on, then we'll measure the results."

When I later asked the Vice President why he thought a new CRM software was necessary, he said that a company had recently presented their software to him and suggested integrating it would help his team sell more. He had been struck by the "silver bullet" syndrome, believing that a single piece of software (or other change) would be the ultimate driver for more sales.

## BUILDING AN UNSTOPPABLE SALES TEAM

Around the age of 13, like many boys my age, I literally couldn't get enough to eat. Fortunately, my mother spent weekends cooking and freezing various baked goodies, which I would slowly consume from our deep freezer. However, she always seemed surprised that half as many baked goods were in a container as she had initially packed. Not sure why that would have been.

One day, after craving some peanut butter cookies, I realized that I had eaten the last one about a week prior. Determined to satisfy my craving, I tried eating peanut butter on a spoon, to no avail. As I grabbed the jar for another spoonful, I noticed a peanut butter cookie recipe on the back and decided that making my own was a good idea despite never having done so.

I quickly began throwing ingredients into a bowl and started mixing. As I mixed, I quickly found that the peanut butter was breaking apart and not sticking to itself to form the cookie. I decided to drop chunks of my peanut butter concoction on a baking tray and waited patiently for the 17 minutes to pass. I could almost taste those cookies.

Unfortunately, after removing the cookies from the oven, I realized that my small peanut butter chunks had remained and looked nothing like a cookie. I realized that I had inadvertently forgotten to add an egg when I returned to the recipe. A minor oversight, but the result was not satisfying my craving. Never one to give up, I attempted a second batch, ensuring I included an egg this time. The texture seemed much better than the first batch and convinced this time I would be successful; I began placing spoonsful of the batter on a freshly cleaned baking sheet. Wanting to compensate for the tiny chunks I had previously cooked, I decided that the single spoonful of peanut butter was not enough to result in a decent-sized cookie, so I used two spoonsful of batter rather than the one.

The result? As the cookies baked, they grew to a size that filled the entire cookie sheet. So, I ended up with one giant peanut butter cookie.

Building your unstoppable sales team is like baking the perfect peanut butter cookie. You will need to introduce several vital components and do so in a specific order. If you don't, you'll wind up with something that may resemble a strong sales team, but like my cookies, they won't meet your expectations.

There are many components to an unstoppable sales team as we'll discuss throughout this book. The components form the foundation upon which you can improve and accelerate performance. Moreover, they are dynamic rather than static. Although you should work progressively through each stage, you can always revert to earlier stages if circumstances demand. For example, new hires, new technology, new markets, or new divisions can often require changes to your team's structure or processes.

Let me also be the first to tell you that building an unstoppable sales team is not fast work. It can be difficult at times, take unexpected turns, and will likely challenge how you think and behave as the leader of a sales team. Unlike other books on building high-performing sales teams, I'm not about to suggest you can have your unstoppable sales team up and running within a couple of weeks. It takes time to build a strong team and to evolve as a high performing leader of the team.

The New York Yankees first won the World Series in 1923. They've since grasped the title an additional 26 times, with their last win in 2009. It took years for the team to reach the performance levels necessary to win the World Series. When you consider the significant turnover in players, it's not surprising (although it is disappointing) that they haven't won since 2009. The Unstoppable Team Framework provides you with all the steps and resources necessary to build an unstoppable sales team, regardless of where you're starting or what changes may lie ahead. Follow this formula and you'll have a winning team that keeps winning. Something the Yankees have lost sight of in recent years.

Before we go too much farther, let me explain my earlier comment about how much time you should expect it to take to build a sales team of unstoppable proportions.

## YOU'RE IN A MARATHON, NOT A SPRINT

Nearly a decade ago, I began working with an organization to build its unstoppable sales team. The Director was desperate after trying multiple other strategies to get her team to work more effectively and generate the sales she expected. After several months of working with the team, we made several significant changes, including changing how the couple communicated, using technology to improve their productivity, and working through several process changes to drive more consistent performance. Within 6 months, the team had nearly doubled their results, with higher collaboration, camaraderie, and sales. Additionally, we put mechanisms in place that we'll discuss in this book that dramatically reduced conflict among the team and resulted in the Director spending significantly less time working with the team, resulting in more time available to work on her other priorities.

My point is simple. Can you build an unstoppable sales team in relatively short order, whose performance will continue to improve over time, increasing your sales results and demanding less time? Absolutely.

However, is it possible it might take you months or even years to have the team reach unstoppable levels of performance? It might. It really depends on where your team is at presently, and the degree of effort you'll be able to expend in implementing my recommendations. The more time you dedicate now, the less time it will take to experience your expected results.

Why might it take you longer? One simple word. Change. Success in any endeavor will require change, and the degree and speed of which you are willing and able to introduce the changes necessary to build your team will determine how quickly you experience results.

While recently watching my oldest son play hockey, another parent from his team mentioned how Matthew was so quick on his skates, often skating around most of the other players as he rushed the other team's net. I chuckled as I recalled his early days of skating, only 6 years earlier, where he would lay on the ice and make snow angels, with absolutely no motivation to skate. Why such a dramatic swing from the only kid not skating to one of the fastest skaters on his team? Change. We began sending Matthew to power skating lessons; hockey schools; and encouraged him to work hard at his skating. Both my wife and I were willing to put in the time and money to try and help him. Additionally, he was amendable to the changes we introduced and continued to work hard to improve his skating. Today he is well on his way to being unstoppable on the ice, although truth be told baseball is his real passion.

I can tell you from experience the difference between excellent and unstoppable may only be a matter of introducing and adopting changes. Of course, the changes and the degree to which the changes will impact day to day will vary for each team, but the difference is what stands between you and the sales team you desire.

## STORIES FROM THE SALES FLOOR

A client of mine in the insurance industry has been slowly acquiring other branches. Initially, his approach was to find branches in a small market with growth potential that were profitable. He would then acquire them, rebrand them, and continue to look for the next acquisition opportunity. After a while, however, he recognized that some branches sold more in a smaller market than others.

While discussing his observations one day, I suggested that he needed to bring the sales teams together regularly to discuss what was working. "Think of it as a sales team brainstorming session," I suggested. When he asked how this might help, I responded, "it's simple. Sales professionals are competitive, and when they hear about the successes others have, it motivates them to try new approaches out for themselves."

He began bringing the teams together several times a year, using the time to update them on new acquisitions and other product and company updates. However, the underlying goal was to get the teams to share what's working in their market and help share best practices. Within a year of introducing these meetings, his sales had grown by double digits, without any other changes.

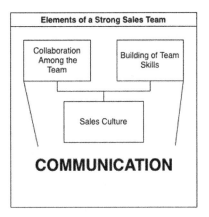

**FIGURE 1.1**
The elements of a strong sales team.

The kinds of changes you're likely to encounter will differ from what you expect. Sure, you're going to make changes in internal and external communications, processes, skills, and technology, but there are other deep-rooted changes you'll need to address. Most commonly these will fall into the areas of sales culture, team collaboration, and skills building (Figure 1.1).

These three areas determine your sales team's ability to reach unstoppable levels and you'll find them referred to several times throughout this book. Furthermore, they are the foundation upon which you'll build your team, as any instability or gaps here will lead to your entire effort unraveling.

When we built a new garage a few years ago, I initially focused on garage size and construction. Next, I focused on whether we'd use 2 × 4 or 2 × 6 walls to build the roof or order pre-built trusses. After meeting with a builder to discuss our plans, he asked how we planned to construct the foundation. I thought about it for a minute, then said, "well, we will use concrete." He laughed and told us to call after we had a foundation in place. Although I was frustrated with his response, I realized why the contractor laughed when we met with a concrete foundation expert.

Upon meeting with the foundation expert, he quickly extinguished my idea of a simple concrete slab. Instead, he informed us of several other vital steps we'd need to take, which required more time and money. For example, we would need to pour footings before the floor, add a re-bar to reinforce the base, and add insulation if we expected the floor to maintain heat. When I told him we were going to pour a slab, he laughed (wondering if there is a trend here?) and suggested a simple slab would crumble like a deck of cards at the first sign of frost or heavy snow load on the roof.

You get my point. Without a strong and adequately constructed foundation, all efforts you put into building your sales team will be futile.

## SCALE SALES FASTER STARTING FROM WHERE YOU ARE RIGHT NOW

It bears mentioning that if you don't put effort into building up your sales team, you'll likely continue to lose top talent and struggle to meet sales targets. So, like my parents used to say, before a challenging exam, you need to "put in the work" if you want to see results.

But don't let this deter you. You won't need to wait until you have worked through all eight components before you experience higher sales. It's the opposite. Once you start building your sales team, you'll see immediate results.

However, there's another bonus to rolling up your sleeves and working to build the team. You can scale your sales much faster. Why? Because you're starting with a team that knows you, your company, its market, competitors, and past practices. Starting from where you are, with what you have, already puts you well out in front of those who pick up this book and are starting to build a new sales team. Sure, your employees might not all be at the levels you want them to be, and there may be some debate among the troops but, fear not, you are in good hands and in the best possible position to accelerate your journey to building an unstoppable team.

Referring to my earlier mention around my oldest son playing hockey, he moves up a division every 2 years as he ages. What this means is that in some years, depending on the age of the kids he plays with, most of his team from the previous year is retained, whereas other years, he might be joining a team that is almost made up entirely of new, and not familiar with each other, players.

Which of these two teams wins more games? It's always the team that retains most of its players as they have familiarity with the game, rules, umpires, and, most importantly, with each other. They know and play to each other's strengths. Moreover, they know the plays that the coach expects to see and the feedback he'll provide. So, in essence, starting with what you have gives you most of the foundational elements we described earlier, with the benefits of knowing what you're selling, who you're selling it to, and who else is selling something similar.

With this said, let's jump into building your unstoppable sales team. In Chapter 2, we'll get started with the proper structure.

# 2

## Your Sales Team's Greatest Challenge

The most difficult thing is the decision to act, the rest is merely tenacity.

**Amelia Earhart**
*American Aviator*

### IT'S BECOMING MORE DIFFICULT FOR YOUR BUYER TO BUY

My first full-time job was at a local A&P grocery store, stocking shelves and packing groceries for customers. Between 11:30 pm and 8:00 am each day, the store would close so that a small group of employees, referring to themselves as "the graveyard crew," would replenish shelves, unpacking boxes and adding stock to empty shelves. Each employee was assigned several aisles to stock and face (a term that refers to pulling stock forward so that the aisle appears full).

After working at A&P for a couple of years, I had the chance to work on a Friday midnight shift, which I gladly did. The shift premium, which I recall was $1 per hour, was nice, but what I enjoyed even more was that I could spend some time early Friday evening with friends, then go to work, return home Saturday morning around 8:15 am, sleep until noon, and then I was good to go for the day. Before I began working the Friday midnight shift, I typically worked Saturdays from 8:30 am to 4:00 pm, so having my Saturday afternoons back, all while making a premium wage, seemed like the perfect solution for a teenager eager to spend time with friends.

DOI: 10.4324/9781003348610-3

When I walk through that same A&P store today, now branded Metro, I'm dumbfounded when I walk down aisle #1, what was aptly referred to on the midnight shift as the cereal aisle. When I once stocked this aisle on a Friday midnight shift, there were rows and rows of the same cereal brands, which at the time included Cheerios, Rice Krispies, Cornflakes, and others. Cheerios, as an example, came in two flavors, regular and honey nut, with three different packaging sizes for each. These included small, medium, and larger boxes often referred to as the Family Pack.

Have you walked down a cereal aisle in your local grocery store lately? If you haven't, try it and look closely at the number of flavors of Cheerios. Recognizing that all stores might not stock every flavor of Cheerios, by my last check, there were 16 different flavors.[1] These flavors come in various sizes as well, so you can imagine the area required just to stock cheerios.

Cheerios is only an example. Walk any aisle of a grocery store today. You'll find that many typical food brands have expanded the options they offer, including different flavors and sizes options. In addition, several new brands have emerged in the last 30 years, including gluten-free and vegan options. The list goes on.

Buying cereal consists of a steadily increasing number of options to choose from, each having its unique features and benefits, and most having a slightly different price. I'm sure you'd agree that this isn't limited to cereal. Cars, toilet paper, vacation packages, and even television have only increased in the number of options to choose from in the last decade, and the rate of these changes is only increasing. For example, when I was young, my grandparents, who lived in the country and used an antenna to tune into television stations, had three channels to watch. Today, we've got a wide array of streaming services like Netflix, Prime, and Disney, each with dozens of channels and hundreds of shows. Funny how it's challenging to find something good to watch, isn't it?

Faced with a growing number of options to choose from, our response as consumers is what you might expect:

- We spend more time researching to determine the "best fit" option for us.
- We seek out opportunities to test and trail various options before fully committing to buy.
- We delay our decision until the choice becomes apparent, or we must choose.
- When we do decide, we can become frustrated when we believe it's not the best choice for us, blaming the seller for misleading us (and often taking to social media and other channels to complain).

These examples of likely responses to a growing number of options are not limited to us as consumers. For example, a recent Gartner study[2] discussing how B2B sales has changed suggests that it's becoming increasingly difficult for buyers to make a buying decision.

The study also highlights several other points that have a direct influence on a buyer's ability to buy, including:

- More information is available to research (i.e., websites, social media, etc.).
- Information is more easily accessible (i.e., increasing use of mobile phones).
- Decisions involve groups or buying teams rather than a single individual.

The results of these changes are like what you might find in the cereal aisle of your local grocery store. People spend time before they shop looking at the different options and pricing (which is part of the reason online grocery shopping is increasing in popularity). Additionally, you'll notice more people standing in the aisle reading packaging before they buy.

So what, you might ask, is the impact of this overwhelming amount of information and options on today's sales professionals?

First, buyers are more discerning, so pitching a product or service has evolved to understand their unique needs and perspectives (influenced by the information received and consumed).

The ability to demonstrate a clear understanding of the buyer's unique situation (even if it's not all that unique) has become paramount to making a buy decision.

Addressing and navigating the broader buying team, those who directly and indirectly influence the sales, including flushing out and effectively responding to their individual questions and concerns, has become an essential skill.

Lastly, *buyer experience* throughout the sales process and even before they buy has become a measure for buyers as to whether the seller has their best interests in mind (and whether they will buy again).

As a result of above, selling is becoming more challenging. The days of traveling the globe, taking your buyer for lunch, and closing the deal over cocktails are becoming more the exception rather than the norm.

Instead, historical sales techniques such as prospecting, discovery, presentation, and closing have all changed. The continued advancement of technology to aid the sales process, along with the need to increasingly collaborate internally to satisfy the buying decision influencers have made being a "lone wolf" in sales obsolete.

## THE DAWN OF BUYER-CENTRIC SELLING

My wife and I were recently looking at purchasing a new awning for our deck. We'd been looking at several options over the years, all of which had their pros and cons. Our deck, on the West side of our home, gets direct sunlight from about 2 pm to 8 pm during the summer months. Although we love the sunshine, a hot, humid day can make sitting out for any length of time almost unbearable.

We've considered building a small roof over our deck; however, it seems too permanent and would limit our ability to get any sun at all (also blocking sunshine from entering our house through nearby windows). We've also looked at retractable awnings and umbrellas at local hardware stores; however, our area is extremely windy, and we've been concerned this type of awning might become damaged easily. When we visited a patio store that specializes in a wide variety of covered structures, we were able to identify the best options considering all these variables we were considering.

The options we found included temporary structures that can convert to sunrooms, heavy-duty awnings that can withstand wind gusts well above what we experience, and permanent structures that attach directly to our home but include skylights to let in sunshine.

After visiting the store, we spent time reflecting on our options and then proceeded to purchase what we needed from an online store, which sold directly to consumers and had lower prices. You might wonder why we didn't buy from the store we visited. The answer is the same reason most B2B buyers seek more self-serve options.

### Self-Serve

We have become, as individuals, accustomed to purchasing products and services online. From pest control to new cars to furniture. Our personal preferences as consumers translate directly into our behaviors for engaging with sales in a working environment.

Considering our earlier discussion on how buyers spend more time researching and less interacting with sales, self-serve options make sense, further influencing today's sales professional role.

Our personal preferences have always influenced our choices for how we work.

In 2004, I received my first BlackBerry™ for work after requesting the President to provide one, allowing me to stay connected with my team and senior leadership while traveling. Like many, I already had my BlackBerry™, so my personal preferences for communication influenced my desire for similar communication methods at work.

A recent study by TrustRadius[3] confirms this, finding that nearly 100% of B2B buyers want self-service options as part of or included in the buying process.

Do self-service demands eliminate the need for sales professionals? Some industries, such as IT and E-commerce, would suggest so. Still, it's more an evolution of the role of a sales professional, transitioning from a Sales Professional to a Sales Concierge, with the primary goal of assisting buyers in navigating their buying journey. More on this transition in subsequent chapters.

For now, consider that your buyers' continued demand for more self-serve options will require a shift in how your sales team approaches their role and how you measure their success.

## TEAM DECISION-MAKING REQUIRES A TEAM APPROACH

When you consider how buyer needs are changing, it becomes apparent that a single salesperson or a team of sales professionals cannot support buyers in their journey by themselves.

For example, can you expect your sales team to be all knowledgeable in every aspect of your product or service?

Is it realistic to think that your sales team can provide all the information a buyer might need during their research?

The short answer is no.

For this reason, we need to build sales teams that collaborate closely with other departments to support our buyers, for example:

Sales must collaborate closely with Marketing to ensure information shared is the information buyers are seeking.

Sales must collaborate with engineering or product development to ensure buyer questions about features and functionality are understood, providing straightforward answers to what is and isn't possible.

Sales must collaborate with operations or production, gaining clarity on lead times and delivery options and ensuring commitments made are commitments kept.

Sales must collaborate within their sales team, bringing in other, more knowledgeable team members to address buyer questions or concerns and to continuously elevate skills.

Although these may seem like obvious steps for any sales professional, in my experience, they aren't. Sales professionals, by nature, are often highly competitive and, in some instances, impatient. The idea of waiting on others to support their prospecting, join in on their presentations, or assist them in closing can be frustrating, especially when buyers are willing to provide little time to sales.

This shift in how today's sales professionals need to operate becomes increasingly challenging when you have a combination of employees and contractors or sales reps as part of your sales team. Although working independently of other functions can provide flexibility in reaching new territories while minimizing overhead, it can also challenge alignment around buyer needs and collaboration in support of those needs.

There are other considerations as well.

In the Gartner study mentioned earlier, buyers need help deciding to buy. As a result, buyers place increasing importance on the ease of making a buying decision and consider it a key factor in determining what their future experience will be.

Unanswered questions, delays in response, or a negative interaction with someone in sales (or even a receptionist who answers the phone) can all result in a lost sale.

Here are the typical criteria buyers use to make buy decisions.

**Questions a Buyer Asks Themselves Before Buying:**

1. Can I easily reach someone in the company to answer my questions?
2. Is the person I connect with knowledgeable about my business and my problems?

3. Does my contact have access to a network of other knowledgeable employees?
4. Does my contact introduce me/my team to other internal experts?
5. How responsive is this company to my inquiries?
6. What will my experience be working with this company?
7. Does my contact make me feel like a welcome guest or an annoying pest?
8. When my question is urgent, does the company respond with urgency?
9. How willing is the company to customize its offering to meet my needs?
10. Does my contact in sales seem like a good fit to work with our team?

There are other questions; however, in my experience, these are the most common.

Some of the most successful companies I know today ensure they have a group whose main role is to support the sales team in educating and addressing buyer needs, inquiries, and questions.

I recently worked with the sales team at a manufacturer of mining equipment. Although the sales team is the face of the company to its customers, many initial meetings, customer presentations, and demonstrations involve other key players, including the Owner, General Manager, VP of Operations, and other team members.

The sales team understands that today's buyers are looking for a team who can support their needs, not just a salesperson who passes them over once the contract is signed.

## INFORMATION OVERLOAD: GETTING THE RIGHT INFORMATION AT THE RIGHT TIME

By this point, you might be thinking that ramping up the supply of information, on your blog, in annual reports, through marketing brochures, or business cards, is something you need to consider if today's buyers are spending so much time of their time researching (you shouldn't carry business cards by the way. If you're unsure as to why, read my book *The Unstoppable Sales Machine*).

More information won't hurt, but you can't reasonably expect your sales team to keep up with the barrage of information you may be sharing. For this reason, building strong internal and external collaborations is key to ensuring your sales team can provide meaningful information and answers to your buyers when requested.

Simply put, a sales professional only needs some of the answers some of the time. This, coupled with a strong network of internal experts and external partners, will position them to provide the information your buyers need during their journey.

I refer to this as building your Sales Information Network or SIN for short.

The most common parties to include are part of your SIN include the following:

- Marketing for market intelligence and competitive information
- Engineering or Development for details on specifications or functionality
- Operations or Production for information on product quality and delivery
- External Vendors or Suppliers for information on supply and specification
- Existing Customers for References and Testimonials

Building an SIN and connecting your sales team with the internal and external relationships to support the questions from your buyer and their teams will help address and inform your buyer's decisions while avoiding overwhelm for your sales team.

If you don't build a SIN for your sales team, you are at risk of sales attempting to become "experts" in your product or service. That might sound good initially, but in my experience, left to their own devices a sales professional will take one of the following approaches to equip themselves with "enough" information about your product or service:

1. They spend *too much time* attempting to research and understand all the information about your product or service to be "prepared" for interactions with your prospects.
2. They become "stuck," unable to decide what information to share (often referred to as analysis paralysis) due to information overwhelm.

3. They skip referencing the information all together as it's deemed as impossible to become acquainted with or explain to the buyer clearly.

Remember, your SIN is meant to support sales without them believing they need to become knowledge experts for your product or service. Additionally, a SIN will ensure your sales team have a support network of experts they can call upon, to address the questions and build relationships with the buyer and their team.

## MASTER OF ONE TRADE; JACK OF NONE

Aside from the confusion that too much information can cause buyers, it creates confusion for sales professionals. Too much information can influence even the most skilled sales professionals to "present" rather than "listen," to "speak" rather than "ask," or to "rush the sales process," rather than focus on "building a relationship."

As the old saying goes, a confused buyer never buys.

From a buyer's perspective, the expectation is that sales will not have all of the answers, but rather, they can quickly access them. In our studies, we've found that trust between a buyer and a sales professional diminishes when sales do not bring other experts into the sales conversation. Another reason building your SIN is so crucial.

However there's a bigger problem at play.

Most sales professionals, particularly those who are new, believe that they must have all the answers. As a result, they often spend excessive time researching and consuming information, thinking that this is the only way to achieve success.

Unstoppable sales teams are equipped with enough information to support their competitive advantage complimented with a network of subject matter experts (your SIN), with the confidence to introduce them during the sales process to answer any questions the buyer, or buyer's teams may have.

Rather than focus on being the most informed person in the room, unstoppable sales teams focus on preparing and asking questions. They learn about the buyer, their needs, and their objectives. They prioritize asking the right questions at the right time, directing their buyer toward their product or service rather than overwhelming them with more information, which can often result in confusion.

In other words, building an unstoppable sales team means you ensure your sales team are masters of understanding by asking good questions, not experts in presenting information that the buyer can access through other, more informed means.

To this point, we've discussed how today's buyers' expectations around the buying process have changed. Additionally, we touched on the challenges they face in navigating an often-overwhelming amount of information; and how sales teams can be better prepared to assist buyers in this journey, creating more opportunities and closing more deals.

In the next chapter, we'll discuss building a strong sales team to support your buyer's needs, increasing the number of leads, the sale velocity, and the close ratio.

### UNSTOPPABLE SALES TEAM ACTION STEPS

1. Assess how convenient it is for your buyer to buy from your team. Where can you make improvements?
2. What individuals or departments need to be part of your SIN? Select and educate these individuals on their role as part of the sales process.
3. Work with your sales team to begin introducing members of your SIN when they need them. Educate members of your SIN on their role and how they can add value to the sales conversation.
4. Pilot your SIN and get feedback from buyers and customers on what you can improve upon for the next time.

For a worksheet to identify and develop your own SIN, see www.unstoppablesales.team

# 3

## *Why Selling Has Become a Team Sport*

… We win as a team, and every individual is better if we are part of the team.

**Fernando Torres**
*Spanish Football Manager*

Whether you have a sales team consisting of 2 or 200 salespeople, focusing your time and energy on building your team will net you more sales results than focusing on any single individual within the team.

For example, many sales leaders focus their time working one-to-one with their sales team, attempting to build competition amongst the group. In reality individuals learn better as a team, so isolating team members only serves to diminish learning and, in some situations, builds animosity or jealousy between team members.

You might wonder, "how can spending most of my time with poor performers be a disservice to the rest of the sales team?"

Simple.

Leading an unstoppable sales team requires balancing our time as leaders in building the right mix of learning for group members. We need to develop what I refer to as healthy dependence *and* independence for everyone on our team. Doing so means providing them with the skills, knowledge, and confidence to be independent while ensuring that the team provides them with support, encouragement, and ongoing skills reinforcement that will help them continue to learn and grow. Creating this kind of environment means that, as leaders, we must divide our time correctly among the team and the members.

Sounds easy enough.

DOI: 10.4324/9781003348610-4

## BEING A LONE WOLF IS JUST LONELY

When I had my first sales job, my sales manager made it clear he had only one goal. He wanted us to sell as many products as possible at the highest profit margin. Therefore, we were encouraged to work independently. The only time we interacted as a team was when the sales manager shared new product information or new promotions. Otherwise, everything was on a one-to-one basis with our manager, including:

- Watching training videos by ourselves in the lunchroom.
- Setting our monthly sales targets one on one with the sales manager.
- Getting feedback on how we were performing.
- Sharing details of a successful high-margin sale.
- Asking questions about new promotions to help us better present to our customers.

It was as if we were learning in a bubble, unable to get feedback from our peers on what worked for them. Additionally, it created an environment of animosity. It wasn't uncommon for the sales manager to challenge us to sell more than our co-workers.

I recall on one Saturday in particular, there hadn't been any customers stopping by, and I was having difficulty reaching anyone on the telephone (which can often be the case during warm summer Saturdays). I was becoming frustrated as it had been a couple of weeks since I last sold anything, so I approached my manager to ask for his opinion.

"Is it just me, or does it seem like everyone is on vacation right now?" I asked. "What do you mean?" asked my manager. Considering it was late July, I presumed many might be away on vacation and, therefore, difficult to reach.

He continued, "Doug just sold three cars this morning, and Sarah sold two last week," was his response. "Keep working the phones and try calling your family and friends," was his advice.

Not to suggest the advice he provided me was inaccurate; it wasn't. But what do you think I walked away from that experience thinking? To be blunt, it created animosity toward both Doug and Sarah.

Old-school thinking in sales suggests we need to isolate members of the sales team to encourage healthy competition. Although it might create some competition, it's rarely healthy. Instead, we need to ensure there is a balance of both independence and dependence. The dependence most commonly being a healthy dependance and desire to collaborate with the team.

**10 Reasons Why Your Sales Team Needs to Collaborate:**

1. Each team member can learn from the ideas and experiences of others.
2. More senior sales professionals can mentor new team members.
3. Mistakes avoid being repeated by those less experienced.
4. The team quickly adopts new sales techniques.
5. New employees get up to speed rapidly on critical skills and selling strategies.
6. Changes in the marketplace are swiftly recognized, allowing for rapid response.
7. Innovative selling strategies get tested before implementation.
8. Changes in the competitive landscape are quickly identified.
9. Product or service problems and solutions and opportunities are broadly shared and recognized.
10. Employee retention increases as team members feel like part of something bigger.

## TOP SALES PERFORMERS ARE ATTRACTED TO STRONG SALES TEAMS

There's another reason why building a strong sales team is our priority over focusing on strong performers within the team, particularly in today's relatively tight job market. It's because strong sales performers are attracted to strong teams.

I've written previously about my oldest son Matthew. He's long been a baseball fanatic, studying baseball stats, watching every Toronto Blue Jays game he can, and repeatedly practicing in our yard, from hitting to pitching.

About a year ago, he switched to a new baseball team, wanting to move from the slow pitch (the crazy fast underhand wind-up pitching that is commonplace in our area) to a fastball team (overhand pitching, like what you'll find online). His reason, of course, was that they only play fastball in the MLB, a goal of his.

While playing in the new league, he had the opportunity to pitch several times and was a natural. After a season of sharing the mound with a few of his teammates, he became known for being accurate and fast—two critical ingredients to any good pitcher.

Matthew studied baseball pitchers for the next year almost obsessively. He practiced his aim and experimented with various pitches against the side of our garage. As the new season approached, Matthew made it clear he was hopeful of joining the "Select" team, a smaller group of baseball teams that are considered a more advanced league. His motivations were to follow in the footsteps of one of his teammates, who in the previous year had played on Matthews's regular and select teams and encouraged Matthew to do the same.

Fortunately, Matthew made the select team in the next season and continues to play in both leagues, pursuing his passion of someday joining the MLB ... you heard it here first.

My son's experience is like what occurs among top-performing sales professionals. They seek to join organizations that have strong sales teams. Sales, like sports, are competitive, and those at the top of their game are naturally competitive. Therefore, you'll often find many top-performing sales professionals were previously involved in or may still be involved in competitive sports.

**Reasons Why Strong Sales Performers Seek Out Strong Sales Teams:**

1. They find solace in healthy competition and seek it out.
2. They want to be a key player in a strong team which bolsters their ego.
3. They are attracted to peer-level interactions, seeking others with skills that are similar to theirs.
4. They seek out relationships with those who complement their existing skills and who have achieved greatness in areas in which they want to improve.
5. They believe their skills (and time) are better spent investing it with those who perform at high (rather than low) levels.

Those who enter the sales profession willingly, often do so because they have a desire to control their own success—referred to as an internal locus of control.

Julian B. Rotter first developed the concept of locus of control in 1954.[4] Rotter defined "Locus of Control" as the degree of control to which people believe they have, as opposed to external forces controlling the outcomes of events in their life. There are two loci that any one person can have:

**Internal locus of control (ILC):** the belief that one can control the factors influencing one's life.

**External locus of control (ELC):** the belief that factors outside one's influence control life; fate or chance controls one's life.

## HOW LOCUS OF CONTROL INFLUENCES A SALESPERSON'S BELIEFS AND BEHAVIORS

Let's look at a common set of circumstances that a salesperson might face, then provide some examples of how a different locus of control can influence the perception of these circumstances and the degree to which they can control, improve upon, or avoid them altogether.

| Circumstances or Situation | Belief: Internal LOC | Belief: External LOC |
|---|---|---|
| Unable to get a meeting with a prospective buyer. | Buyers are too distracted and too busy to meet with me. | I just haven't found a good enough reason to convince buyers to meet with me yet. |
| Consistently loosing sales due to a price objection. | The price of our products or services are too high for what buyers are willing to pay. | I need to develop a better response to pricing objections, demonstrating a clear return on investment. |
| Cold calling doesn't work and making outreach phone calls hasn't resulted in a meeting. | Cold calling is old school; it doesn't work, and people find it annoying when I call. | Cold calling is still one of the best ways to connect with buyers. I need to test some methods to use it more effectively. |
| My buyers don't want to meet face-to-face anymore. | The pandemic resulted in everyone working from home; buyers aren't in their offices anymore, so I can't visit them. | Some of my buyers are working from home, but of those many are still happy to connect at local coffee shops or restaurants for meetings. |
| People I meet with haven't heard of us or our products. | Our marketing isn't effective and until we get better marketing, I won't get any new leads. | Our marketing may not be strong, but considering most people buy from those they know, like, and trust, I need to test new methods to get in front of my ideal buyers. |

You can easily see how an ELC is one of the critical factors in building a strong sales mindset and fundamental to building a strong sales team. An ELC is built when those on your sales team are exposed to others who have an ELC. It challenges their mindset and can influence a shift in how they view the challenges they are facing.

This said, there's something even more important to consider regarding the locus of control of those on your sales team.

Like attracts like, meaning when you build a sales team that consists of sales professionals who, for the most part, want to be part of the team and have an ELC, then you have an environment that will help you attract more of the same type of sales professional.

Alternatively, if you inherit a sales team in which many employees appear to have an internal locus of control, their only reason for being there is the money, to have your companies name on their resume, or to gain experience they'll take elsewhere, then the same rule applies. Your environment (in this case a toxic one) is likely to attract more of the same kinds of sales professionals, making it difficult to retain any good employees and almost impossible to build an unstoppable sales team.

If any of this last scenario sounds familiar, have no fear. Whether the majority of your sales team's has an internal or ELC is less important than the type of learning environment you create. You'll just need to work harder to gain the attention and interest of those with an internal locus of control in participating in a learning environment.

## CREATE AN ENVIRONMENT RIPE FOR LEARNING

Aside from locus of control, you can quickly elevate the performance of your sales team when you create an environment ripe for learning. For example, having team members consistently share "what's working now" strategies they are having success applying can create an environment where there is consistent exposure to a never-ending flow of new ideas.

The learning you provide can come from other sources, including formal education, sales training, sales coaching, customer feedback interviews, and various other sources. The key is to create an environment in which team members gain exposure to various ideas, information, strategies, techniques, and observations.

The keys then to creating this kind of environment are:

- Variety of information, ideas, and strategies
- Consistent exposure
- Internal and external sources
- Open sharing and encouragement

There will be differences for each individual on your team relative to their willingness to adopt, apply, and share best practices; however, you can heavily influence these factors if you create an environment ripe for learning. You *can* teach an old dog new tricks; it just takes a little patience.

Malcome Shepherd Knowles, an American educator, used the term andradology (the concept of experiential learning) as synonymous with adult education.[5] Knowles made five assumptions about the characteristics of adult learners, namely:

1. Self-concept: How a person's self-concept shifts from being a dependent personality toward being self-directed.
2. Adult learner experience: As a person matures, they accumulate a growing reservoir of experience that becomes an increasing resource for learning.
3. Readiness to learn: As a person matures, their willingness to learn becomes increasingly oriented toward the developmental tasks of their social roles.
4. Orientation to learning: As a person matures, their perspective changes from postponed application of knowledge to immediacy of application.
5. Motivation to learn: As a person matures, the motivation to learn is internal.

Knowles confirms that although the locus of control for every member of your sales team may not be external, with the proper environment, we can ensure consistent learning and application of new skills if we create the right environment for our sales team.

When I speak at conferences, I always incorporate a group activity, even if my talk is only for 45 minutes. My purpose in doing so is to ensure that the audience, made up of adults, can discuss each other's experiences with the techniques and strategies shared. For example, you might wonder if I suggest it takes only two touchpoints to reach today's buyer rather than the average of 12 that many so-called experts suggest. Even if I could share a relevant study or example, your experience might suggest otherwise. However, let's suppose I have others in the audience who can share a similar experience. In that case, your willingness to accept the chance that reaching a new prospect after two touchpoints is possible increases.

As a sales leader, you should take the same approach. Focus on creating an environment ripe for learning, which will increase the adoption of new ideas and strategies, and ultimately improve the sales performance within the team.

Figure 3.1 depicts when to incorporate experiential learning for your sales team.

Several years after our two sons were born, my wife wanted to return to work part-time. She spent several months looking at open positions and discussing whether they might fit. Her conclusion, which I agreed with, is that she is very good with children and decided to accept a part-time role assisting in an after-school program.

After working in the role for only a month, her employer approached her and asked if she had ever considered attaining her RECE (Registered Early Childhood Educator) designation.

| Priority for Application of Experiential Learning | | | |
|---|---|---|---|
| | New Employee | Experienced Employee | Senior Employee |
| New Process | HIGH | MEDIUM | LOW |
| New Technology | HIGH | HIGH | HIGH |
| New Product/Service | MEDIUM | MEDIUM | LOW |

**FIGURE 3.1**
Incorporating experiential learning for your sales team.

Dreading the thought of returning to college, my wife learned of a local program blended in-class and workplace learning. She decided to pursue the program because it offered an environment of both information and education, combined with learning from her peers on the job. It created a unique and powerful learning environment. Needless to say, she graduated with honors and quickly became a top performer in her field.

There is another benefit to developing a learning environment for your sales team. It gives members of your team a chance to fail. When we learn through the experiences of others, we can learn from their failures and successes. As a sales leader, encouraging (not discouraging) the trialing of new ideas and sharing what didn't work (just as often as what did work) is a crucial strategy for building a learning environment.

By encouraging your team members to share openly about wins and losses, successes and failures, while challenging each other and applying what they learn, you create an environment in which team members cannot help but learn. Doing so is a key strategy for building your unstoppable sales team.

## YOU'RE SITTING ON A GOLD MINE OF BEST PRACTICES

In the skills development work I do with sales teams globally, there is one belief I have always held. Every sales team is sitting on a gold mine of best practices upon which to build. The key is extracting these best practices and having the rest of the sales team test and adopt these skills as their own.

For example, you may have someone on your sales team who is highly effective in meeting buyers. Others may look up to or even be jealous of this person's ability to get meetings, but they don't have to be. The reality is this individual acquired this skill over time, and as a result, it can easily be shared, dissected for lessons learned, mapped out in terms of best practice, and then shared with and applied by others. When you uncover the perceived hidden talents of each member of your sales team, you unlock a gold mine of new ideas that others can use.

Here are some examples of best practices that may exist within your sales team today that you can easily extract, deconstruct, and then have the rest of your sales team adopt.

- John gets more meetings consistently than anyone else on the sales team.

- Sarah has a higher average closing ratio than anyone else on the sales team.
- Frank can reach more prospects via telephone than anyone else.
- Hailey can prepare virtual presentations that repeatedly win clients.
- Sean can consistently complete five meetings each day while traveling.
- Ruby consistently upsells new customers for higher-value proposals.

This list of best practices is nearly endless, and the more people that exist on your sales team, the greater your ability to extract and share these best practices.

I began using the term "internal best practices" after several years of leading teams across various companies and industries. I wrote about many of these experiences and methods in my seminal book "*The Unstoppable Organization*," which provides the foundation for building a culture committed to finding and serving customers.

Having personally led teams as large as 90 people and as few as three across several different industries, I've learned that I could dramatically speed up the team's adoption of skills (and willingness to do so) if we uncovered existing best practices within the group. Much of my focus with the teams were to have individual members explain and train others on the uniqueness of their approach. This methodology became a primary component of my 90-day plan when I joined any new company and is a crucial component of how I work with clients today to unlock the potential of their sales team and it's a key component of my work with sales teams today.

The good news is that the approach I developed is easily replicable whether your sales team consists of 2 people or 200. Here are the key steps to replicate this process for your sales team.

## SHAWN'S SEVEN-STEP APPROACH FOR SALES TEAMS TO ADOPT INTERNAL BEST PRACTICES

**Step 1:** Identity, in conjunction with your sales team, who has tremendous success in each aspect of your current sales process. Begin discussing the various aspects of prospecting, then transition to discovery, presentation, making proposals, dealing with objections, closing, and post-close support.

**Step 2:** As you explore each of these areas, identify who achieves the best results; what the results are; and then painstakingly have them break down the steps they take to achieve these results.

**Step 3:** Capture the steps individually, as if writing an instruction manual for someone who has never completed the task. Have someone on your team review the notes to ensure they can be understood and replicated.

**Step 4:** Test the completeness of these steps by having the individual walk someone through their process, then have the person learning to review the steps to ensure accuracy. Once complete, capture this information in the form of a sales process, checklist, flowchart, or any other method in which you would typically capture sales processes.

**Step 5:** Roll out the completed steps to the entire sales team, providing them a challenge to review their process in this area and identify the adjustments needed to replicate the new approach. Have each team member report weekly (or bi-weekly) on their progress and results. I recommend incorporating time during an existing sales meeting to review progress, having each team member share their challenges in implementing the new changes and their lessons learned openly. Have the person who shared the best practice in attendance and act as a mentor, providing feedback and advice.

**Step 6:** Based on the team's progress and feedback, make any final adjustments to these new best practices, and capture information for future team training or orientation.

**Step 7:** Repeat this process for each area of your sales process, discussing results and using the person who shared their strategy as a mentor to the others.

Although uncovering best practices from within your sales team is straightforward, there are a few barriers you may encounter to be aware of, namely:

- Those with exceptional results are part of the sales process but need to improve at explaining or helping others understand these processes.
- Those who hold their approaches or techniques closely prefer to keep the secrets to their success private.
- Those who have succeeded despite practicing some destructive behaviors, which you wouldn't want the rest of the team to adopt.

- Animosity among the team when one member has exceptional results in several areas of the sales process.
- Those who become jealous or close-minded to listening or learning from others.

Overcoming any or all of these barriers does require some work. Still, when you, as the sales leader, see yourself as a conduit to this level of learning, connecting each member of your sales team with the best practices of their peers and, in turn, helping each elevate their performance, the effort is worth it. Of course, it requires patience, persistence, and tenacity, but I'm confident you already possess that.

When you consider that best practices already exist among your team, the fastest way to increase your sales teams' results is to extract, dissect, and integrate these best practices with the rest of the team members.

It sounds straightforward enough, but what happens when one person on the sales team achieves results miles above the rest? Are you at risk of them getting bored or frustrated and leaving your team? Worse yet, do they want your job?

That's the topic of our next chapter, so read on!

### UNSTOPPABLE SALES TEAM ACTION STEPS:

1. What are the key areas of your sales process where results of each team member vary significantly?
2. Pick one straight forward process, and then work through the six steps above.
3. Create a routine of sharing successes among the team, and challenge other team members to replicate this success.
4. Tie the application of best practices to quarterly performance, to reinforce the need to adopt new techniques.
5. Reward team members who adopt and achieve new outcomes as a result of this approach.

For your copy of the Unstoppable Sales Team Action Planner, see www. unstoppablesales.team

# 4

## The Foundation of a Winning Sales Team

To succeed, you will soon learn, as I did, the importance of a solid foundation in the basics of education—literacy, both verbal and numerical, and communication skills.

**Alan Greenspan**
*Former Chair of the Federal Reserve of the United States*

Many years ago, I led a sales team of 12 people, each with their own territory. Among the group, several new individuals had joined the organization before I did, and a few had been with the company for over 10 years.

Two individuals had been responsible for most of the business and continued to grow their territories each year. The remaining team members had sporadic success selling the company's products. It became clear that our two top salespeople approached selling very differently and that although they each followed our sales processes, there were nuances to how they sold.

To help those struggling, I organized a meeting with the team, during which I interviewed the two top performers, asking them questions about their approach to selling, how they dealt with hard-to-reach buyers, and how they handled objections own.

The meeting lasted about 4 hours and was a huge hit. Not only did participants learn new ways to sell, but they learned the secrets to their peer's success (making their success seem that much more possible).

There were a few points mentioned that I didn't necessarily agree with, to which I made some clarifications, but overall, their approach and

DOI: 10.4324/9781003348610-5

strategies were sound. Of these messages, one stood out among all that helped the rest of the team and helped me. Both strong performers continuously referenced how long they'd been selling this product and underlined the importance of time. They shared examples of closing prospects they'd been working with for nearly 10 years; and the value of sticking with a prospect despite believing the opportunity was dead.

It was through this experience that it became clear to me that high-performing sales professionals further elevate their team's performance if given the opportunity to share their wisdom and experiences with others. Our goal, then, as we discussed in Chapter 3, is to create an environment where our sales team can learn, share, and thrive, elevating the performance of each and everyone on the team.

Developing this environment requires creating a foundation for success.

———————

## SELLING IS COMPETITIVE; TAKE ADVANTAGE OF IT

Competition often naturally exists when you have more than one person selling the same product or service. Although not everyone is highly competitive by nature, from a behavioral standpoint, many sales professionals tend to have a competitive side that drives them to want to "outsell" their peers or to "win" their next client.

William Marsden,[6] a famous psychologist, credited with forming the basis for what is known as the DiSC behavior model, suggested that the "D" behavior style, which is the behavior that is Dominant and results-focused, is the most competitive behavior.

For our purposes, and as a quick summary, the behavior model hypothesizes that there are four predominant behaviors that any one person can have.

These four behaviors are described as:

D—dominant
I—influential
S—steady
C—conscientious

Having used various assessments over the years with sales teams and leaders, I can tell you that although these tools can shed light on why someone behaves in a particular manner, there are inherent risks. The goal of an assessment is to recognize our strengths to exploit further, not to label our behavior. An assessment is only a minor part of the equation when it comes to an understanding and enhancing the performance of your sales team.

There are companies out there (who remain nameless) that would suggest *their assessment* is everything you need to fully understand your sales team better. Such a statement would be misleading.

Outside of individual behaviors, we also must consider other variables that can impact someone's ability and desire to sell. These include personal experiences, education, thought patterns, social environments, demographics, etc.

Figure 4.1 outlines the phases for building a strong sales team and uncovering the key drivers of Sales Team Culture.

As an example of how our behaviors influence our perceptions consider the following. As a sales leader if believe that all sales professionals are highly competitive (or should be), then it means three things:

1. You are a competitive person yourself (we often presume others have a similar motivation to ourselves).
2. You appreciate members of your team who have the desire to win (and receive your approval) more than others who don't demonstrate this outright.
3. Members of your team who are not naturally competitive are unlikely to be motivated by your leadership, and most likely will eventually leave the team.

**FIGURE 4.1**
Sales team culture drivers.

Although there may be the opportunity to introduce competition individually within the team, as we've discussed in previous chapters, exploiting this can erode the team culture, leading to a "step on everyone to reach the top" mentality.

Our own behaviors styles, according to Marston, inform our personal biases and influence our expectations of others. Just because we as leaders may have biases doesn't mean this is how others are motivated to perform—members of a strong sales team may have similar behaviors to your own (i.e., be direct with prospects, methodical in their prospect research, or extraverted and willing to speak to events in front of prospects), but they will also have their own behaviors. It's through a wide diversity in experience, behaviors, and the resourcefulness of sales team members that we build an unstoppable sales team.

So then every sales team requires a combination of behaviors and experience if they are to be successful. Therefore, the selection of the "best team members" of the group is highly dependent on what they will be selling, who they will be interacting with (i.e., behaviors and expectations of your customers or clients), and the strengths and weaknesses of other team members.

The goal, then, is to create a high-performing sales team rather than a team that consists of high-performing individuals. This approach results in a sales team culture that will both attract top talent and retain them, all while yielding the results every sales leader desires.

How do we create a competitive team that wins together?

## EXPERIENCE TRUMPS THEORY: LEARN BY DOING

In Chapter 3, we discussed the importance of experiential learning as the most effective way for adults to learn. It's the bridge that brings together a team of varying behaviors, needs, and motivations.

This is why any of the sales coaching or development work I do with sales teams focuses on practice and application. I would rather someone walk away from one of my talks or trainings with two or three ideas they'll actually apply than a page full of notes that will eventually be recycled. My goal is not to immerse participants in theory and instruction but rather to get them to act and apply new techniques and methods to gain experience.

After working with sales professionals and sales teams for over 15 years, it's become apparent that once someone uses a new approach or skill and sees new (desired) results, they tend to alter their behaviors to continue achieving the new (desired) results.

When I began my first real sales job in my twenties, it took a couple of months before I made any sales. My peers were all selling cars, yet as the "new guy," I made minor errors, resulting in no sales. However, over time these tiny errors built my experience (and confidence) to the point that my results surpassed that of the other team members, who began asking me for guidance.

Here are some examples those tiny errors and the lessons I learned:

There was a woman who (while driving full-sized Grand Marquis, which she loved) asked to buy a small, compact Pontiac Sunfire. After a test drive, she said she was interested and would call me. Unfortunately, she didn't, and I later found out that she purchased another used Grand Marquis (full-sized car) from a dealership just down the street.

*Lesson learned*: Prospects may know what they think they want; our role in sales is to uncover what they need. Be observant of what they currently drive and make recommendations on cars that are similar.

A man showed up on a motorcycle from outside the area wanting to price on a new full-sized heavy-duty Chevrolet pickup truck. I spent time showing him all the truck's features, and despite his declining a test drive, I shared an "out-the-door" price with him. He said he would come back and was interested, yet I could never reach him again.

*Lesson learned*: Price shoppers want prices, don't waste time providing demos; give them what they want, and if they're interested, you'll know.

There was a time when a gentleman, in to have his car serviced, was sitting patiently in the lobby. I sat down beside him and began talking. He quickly shared that he was having his car serviced and wasn't looking to buy anything. Undeterred, I acknowledged what he had said, and we continued our conversation. Three months later, he called me and ordered a car over the phone, with no negotiation or request for discounts. Instead, he said, "I appreciated our conversation and that you weren't pushing a sale, even though you knew I wasn't buying anything."

*Lesson learned*: Only disqualify people if they are ready to buy today. Eventually, they'll likely need what you sell, so always be building relationships.

You can likely list out dozens, if not hundreds, of your own experiences like these, and despite the frustration that may have resulted, you learned because of these experiences.

Reading, studying, and researching are all critical in becoming high-performing sales professionals, but we learn by doing at the end of the day.

Building an Unstoppable Sales Team requires creating a sales culture that embraces learning by testing and trying new skills, techniques, and strategies. Our studies have shown that many sales professionals will follow their organizations sales process diligently, for fear of being reprimanded or frowned upon if they don't produce the desired sales results. So although having a sales process and practices makes sense, it creates several challenges:

1. It doesn't allow employees to be creative (i.e., exploration of new methods and techniques given someone's personal strengths).
2. Employees can't practice individuality (i.e., adjustments to methods to better align with individual behavioral preferences).
3. It reinforces conformity, which will, over the long term, further stifle creativity and the desire to make adjustments to methods based on changes in buyer behaviors and expectations.

In other words, sales professionals need freedom and flexibility in how they apply sales processes. Although following proven practices to sell makes sense, this needs to account for the individuality of each salesperson.

As you might imagine, environments that emulate the "do it our way or hit the highway" approach in how they expect their sales team to operate are neither motivating enough to keep strong sales performers nor enticing enough to attract new talent. Instead, we need to encourage an environment of improvement, taking a page from successful continuous improvement movement of the nineties. Interestingly, this concept was (and still is) rarely applied to the area of sales.

To be clear, I'm not suggesting you start introducing lean practices or six sigma. Instead, use "continuous improvement" to reinforce the mindset and method with which we lead and motivate our sales teams. Encourage our sales team to learn by doing, applying, and testing new theories and strategies to improve performance further. Then, when they make mistakes, recognize this is all part of the learning journey and encourage them to keep going.

The caveat to this approach is that if you are enabling your sales team to learn by doing (experiential learning), then you'll gain the best result when you apply the following steps:

1. New methods, practices, or creative ideas are discussed as a group, incorporating experience that extends beyond one salesperson and gaining feedback and input from the team as to whether the practice or theory seems to have merit and has an opportunity for success.
2. New processes or procedures are introduced at a micro level to assess their success, sharing findings with the team. The technique (and any improvements) becomes part of the sales process if the results are positive.
3. Changes in process or practice are captured and documented to ensure their consistent application across the team. Examples include written procedures and differences in how technology is applied or included as an agenda element in regular team meetings or discussions.

So the keys to forming a foundation for your unstoppable sales team are as follows:

1. Create an environment where your sales team feels comfortable and confident in sharing new strategies and ideas.
2. Provide your team with the opportunity to test and trial new methods without fear, reprimand, or embarrassment.
3. Ensure the team openly shares their successes or lessons learned with other team members.
4. New steps or lessons learned are then incorporated into existing practices or processes to ensure the sales team consistently uses them.

My Sales Team Performance Framework (Figure 4.2) shows how the learn-by-doing practice should be incorporated to build your Unstoppable Sales Team.

Creating an environment such as the one described above is motivating to a sales team. They have the processes that, if followed, have historically

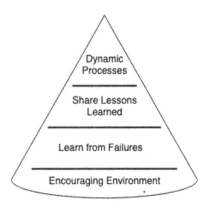

**FIGURE 4.2**
Sales team performance framework.

led to solid sales results, but they also can test and trial new theories, first discussed with their team for input and feedback.

The indirect result is both consistently improving sales results for the entire team and an encouraging environment where employees believe their ideas are important and have a platform to share them within. Although the learn-by-doing approach to sales leadership can indirectly motivate sales teams to learn from new ideas and methods, there's more to consider.

## MOTIVATION IS INSIDE OUT AND OUTSIDE IN

When building your unstoppable sales team, motivation is a critical tool a sales leader has at their disposal. Get motivation right, and your team will outsell and outwork their competition; if you get it wrong, you'll need help to make sales and keep your people.

Motivation itself is a funny thing. When it comes to motivating sales professionals or the teams they are on, what motivates one individual may differ significantly from another. For example, the opportunity for advancement might drive you to outperform your team members, whereas the chance for higher commissions might motivate your teammate.

Along the same lines, what motivates us as sales leaders might not motivate our sales team. For this reason, we need to think about motivation on two levels:

1. Group level motivation: Generating motivation at a group level involves commonly accepted norms. An example of motivation at a group level would be money, as most people work to earn income.
2. Individual level motivation: At an individual level, motivation is based on needs, wants, and desires. Changing someone's title is an example of an individual motivator. Some people care about their title based on their perception of stature, whereas others seek a title only if it comes with other benefits.

Some group-level motivators can also motivate at an individual level. Although money represents motivation at a group level, *how that money is used* (and the reason it is sought) can be very personal. I might support my family, whereas you might work to buy a bigger boat.

By considering motivation at these two levels, we minimize this tendency. We can approach motivation on a much broader level, resulting in a greater chance that our efforts to motivate our sales team will be successful.

Whether you fully consider motivation at these two levels to identify specific motivation strategies and tactics is optional. What is important is that, as sales leaders, we think beyond what we find motivating to motivate others.

If you recognize the importance of motivation to keep your sales team excited and interested in selling, remember this: We can motivate our team only once we understand what motivates everyone. This insight, combined with recognizing what motivates the group, positions us to continuously create motivation that will encourage our sales team and ensure they stick with us over the long term.

We'll dive into the topic of exactly how to motivate your sales team in Chapter 9, but for now, consider that as a sales leader, we need a method that encourages our sales team on both an individual and group basis. Something that is replicable and supports sustained motivation over the long term.

## SUCCESS BREEDS SUCCESS

Sales leaders often attempt to add success to their team rather than create an environment that breeds success. For example:

- They hire or promote a top sales performer.
- They increase bonuses or commissions in specific regions to boost sales.
- They take on key accounts themselves to demonstrate how their employees should behave.

None of these steps breed success; they only attempt to add success where none exists at the team level.

You might ask your sales team to increase their outbound calls by 50%. However, unless they have achieved this in the past or can observe someone else who works at this level (and who they deem to have the same skills, ability, capacity, knowledge, and circumstances as themselves), they will most likely believe it is not achievable.

Instead, we need to bridge our requests, expectations, or requirements for the team to examples of others who can achieve these results and with whom they can relate.

Let's look at some examples:

If you want your sales team to make 100 outbound calls daily (presuming they aren't already), share examples of others from within or outside the team who are consistently making this many calls daily and who work within a similar environment and with similar constraints.

If you want to increase your team's closing ratio, share examples of others closing more deals and selling a similar product or service to a similar prospect working in similar circumstances.

If I want you to get your team to travel more frequently, give examples of others who have desirable lifestyles and responsibilities to theirs and who travel more frequently but make the process enjoyable.

Generating buy-in to new performance levels relies on observations of those who we believe are in similar circumstances to ours and are achieving different (better) outcomes.

We build a learning environment by using examples of others within or outside of the team to whom our team members can relate.

Mia Hamm,[7] a famous American Soccer Player, is known for her quote, "Success Breeds Success." Our role as sales leaders in building an unstoppable sales team requires creating an environment that breeds success. Since success is measured by what we understand to be possible, we must focus our time and energy on creating an environment where members believe higher levels of performance are possible, for example:

- Share individual wins making them relevant to each person on the team.
- Introduce mentoring as a method of developing new skills.
- Encourage employees to test new theories and ideas.
- Provide rewards based on individual capabilities and accomplishments.
- Recognize and reward a willingness to try new practices.

The degree to which we as leaders can create an environment in which our team members can observe and learn from each other, bridging the gap between what everyone believes is possible for themselves, will determine the team's success.

### UNSTOPPABLE SALES TEAM ACTION STEPS:

1. What methods can you introduce to encourage a "learn by doing" culture within your team?
2. How will you ensure that the experience and learnings by different team members are shared with the rest of the group?
3. What are the individual and group motivators are for your sales team?
4. How can you incorporate and use these motivators on a regular basis?
5. How will you encourage other team members to follow your lead and apply these motivators in their interactions with others?

For a copy of your Unstoppable Sales Team Action Planner, see www.unstoppablesales.team

# Part II

# Building Your Unstoppable Sales Team

Since 2009, I've been working with teams globally to elevate their performance. What I've observed during this time is that regardless of the size of your team, the products or services they sell, or their level of success in selling, their level of performance can always be elevated.

The difference between the level of performance your sales team exhibits today and the level of performance you would like them to achieve, is simply a matter of applying the steps laid out over the next few chapters. So, if you're ready to get started, let's dive in!

DOI: 10.4324/9781003348610-6

# 5

## *Where to Begin: Assessing Your Sales Team's Performance*

The journey of a thousand miles begins with one step.

**Lao Tzu**
*Chinese Philosopher*

The starting point for building your unstoppable sales team is to identify their current level of performance. You likely believe your team is underperforming at this point (otherwise, why would you be reading this book)? That said, we need to look at your team's performance in greater depth, assessing several variables of the team and the individuals within it.

Referring to Chapter 4, one of the most significant risks in assessing performance is that we judge the performance of others based on *our* experience or observations, rather than the individual or teams experience and capabilities. For example, if you are a strong closer with a ratio of 90% or greater, you likely find closing a deal is easy and you in turn expect others to be able to achieve similar results.

I call this the Sales Performance Bias. It's the tendency that we, as sales leaders, presume that others are as good as we are at selling and that our experience establishes the baseline of what anyone can achieve. In other words, everyone should be as successful as we are (or as successful as we believe we would be if in their position). Additionally, the longer you remain in a sales leadership role, the less connected you become with the activity, demands and challenges of selling. As a result, we tend to underestimate the degree of effort taken to achieve results.

DOI: 10.4324/9781003348610-7

To overcome the Sales Performance Bias, we need to consider the skills, abilities, and results of each person on our team on an individual level, then contrast them against the following:

1. The performance of others in the same function, activity, or role.
2. The individual's capabilities (i.e., education, experience) as well as those you're comparing them too.
3. Factors beyond the individuals control that have an impact on their abilities (i.e., a down economy, ineffective CRM software, insufficient training, etc.).

Before we dive into discussing the best model for assessing *your* team's performance, let's start by setting a performance baseline against which to measure.

## SETTING A SALES PERFORMANCE BASELINE

I've been riding motorcycles since I was in my early twenties. My first experience was when a friend gave me a ride to high school on the back of his Honda. I fell in love with the experience, and it didn't take long until I bought one of my own.

Before throwing a leg over however, I made the decision to take a motorcycle training course at a local college. Licensing in Ontario for motorcyclists at the time was graduated with three different levels, each with fewer restrictions than the former. By starting my learning in an approved training program, I could skip level one and move directly to level two.

The program began on a Friday evening, covering theories such as motorcycle operation, basic road safety, and an overview of weekend activities. Essentially Saturday was designed to set a baseline for each rider's skill level, allowing riders to be grouped based on their ability and determining the level of instruction necessary. The lower-skilled riders, who had never sat on a motorcycle and were slow to gain confidence, spent the most time with their instructor. At the other end of the spectrum, more skilled riders who had already received their level one license and had been riding on the road for some time spent less time with an instructor.

Throughout the day Saturday, each rider progressed in skills at a different rate. There were some who, by the end of the day Saturday, were still riding at the same pace and speed they had began the day with, noticeably unconfident and uncomfortable riding. On the contrary, some riders had seemingly mastered the art of riding, quickly gaining new skills and confidence. Fortunately, I was in this group, and you'll be happy to know I passed the program and have been riding, albeit sporadically (children, work, and life can get in the way of time to take a leisurely ride) ever since.

The goal of setting a performance baseline is to create alignment between where you and your employee think they are relative to their existing performance. When agreed upon, you can lay out the pathway to improving performance on an individual basis, making any necessary adjustments, improvements, or changes to cater to everyone on the team. Doing so will help you overcome the Sales Performance Bias.

To build an unstoppable sales team, we'll need to set a performance baseline to identify the various components, tools, development, and experience necessary to elevate your sales team's performance.

When improving the performance of a sales team, there are three essential factors to consider:

1. Every individual possesses a different level of skill, ability, and confidence. As a result, a "baseline" isn't a set level for your entire sales team but rather various stages that accommodate different skill and ability levels.
2. Each skill can have a unique baseline. When we consider the fundamental skills required of our team, we need to determine the baseline for each skill and recognize different employees will be at different levels for each skill. For example, someone who is strong in negotiation may be weak in conversion or closing skills.
3. Everyone develops and adopts new skills and abilities at different speeds. Setting a baseline requires we create pathways to the next level that accommodate these different speeds at which people can learn and apply new skills. You can use something simple to represent three levels: slow, moderate, and advanced.

Figure 5.1 denotes how your performance baseline should accommodate these variables.

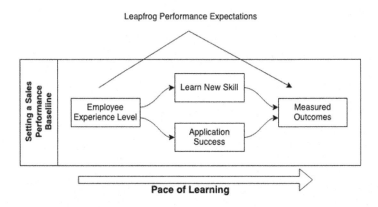

**FIGURE 5.1**
Sales performance baseline.

So, although the performance measures used in the baseline will be common for most of your sales team (i.e., outbound calls), you'll need to avoid creating a single target or standard for each (i.e., having a target of the same number of outbound calls for every person on your team). Then when you measure individual performance, you'll be able to score each person in a much more independent and accurate manner, using this information to create a more personalized (and effective) performance plan.

For example, suppose you expect everyone to make 50 outbound calls to new targets each week. In that case, you'll need to consider the extent to which this is achievable for each person based on their existing book of business and their experience. So, for example, the measure might be as follows:

Outbound calls—junior employee: 50 new targets per week (no or few new accounts)

Outbound calls—experienced: 35 new targets per week (plus nurture existing accounts)

Outbound calls—advanced: 15 new targets per week (plus nurture existing accounts)

As you score your team, reflect upon their existing skills, willingness, and ability to learn, and the speed at which they've proven they can understand and apply new skills. Using your judgment to identify their performance level for each measure, referencing examples to support your thesis. Let me repeat this last part because it's essential IF you want to get buy-in from your team on their assessment. The examples you use MUST support your scoring of their performance; otherwise, it is your opinion which, although it has merit, will need to be more to gain their agreement.

If, for example, you think someone who has worked for you for 5 years is still in the "Junior" category, using the above example, what examples can you share that prove this? For example, you might give examples of how others have a more significant book of business that requires more time to manage; therefore, they are still at a junior level until they gain this same number of accounts. You could also include examples of the experience other employees have outside of a similar job, experiences they have had on the job, etc.

With these points in mind, let's start by formulating your sales team's performance baseline against which you can effectively measure their performance. Again, the goal is to create alignment and, to some extent, agreement with individual team members on their level of performance, and the steps they'll need to take to progress further in their performance. To start formulating your performance baseline, let's focus on the key results measures that you will want to consider developing your performance baseline.

- New leads identified
- New target markets identified
- Leads confirmed
- Leads qualified
- Meetings booked
- Meetings converted to a proposal or quote
- Proposal or quotes generated
- The total value of the proposal or quote
- Speed of overcoming objections
- Time to close a proposal or quotation
- Proposal or quotes won
- Proposal or quotes lost
- Proposal or quotes open

You'll notice how these measures tie directly to a critical element of the sales process. Depending on what you sell, the complexity of your product or service, and the average time to close, there may be additional performance measures to consider. For example, if what you sell is technology based, you'll want to consider other measures, such as the lifetime value of lead (LTV), monthly re-occurring revenue (MRR), and churn.

For a complete list of measures and a Performance Baseline checklist, see www.unstoppablesales.team

Now that we've identified a baseline for the performance of your sales team, let's discuss how the performance baseline will help you identify and isolate poor performance and what to do once you separate it.

## WHY YOU NEED TO ISOLATE POOR PERFORMANCE

Setting a performance baseline allows us to get clear on the level of performance of each person on our sales team, informing the development that will be necessary to further elevate their performance. When you do this for the entire team on an individual basis, it will allow you the chance to identify and isolate performance, informing your next steps in skills development.

Now would be a good time to re-affirm that every employee is NOT capable of becoming a sales superstar, nor will they want to be such, and that's okay. An unstoppable sales team needs a variety of skills sets, behaviors and experience to be effective. As a quick example, if everyone on your team was a superstar bringing in new accounts, chances are your retention and growth of existing accounts would be low. On the contrary, if most of your team members were good at managing current accounts, your influx of new accounts would be low. Increasing your sales (particularly to unstoppable levels – see my book *The Unstoppable Sales Machine* for more insights here) requires you have a blend of talent, all with varying levels of skills and ability, in roles that support your continued growth.

Setting a performance baseline as outlined earlier, allows you to create a standard measurement tool for the entire team that accounts for each individual and their current experience, capability, experience, etc. You can isolate poor performance very quickly without incorporating a "gut feel" into the equation. Your instinct as to whether someone will be a good fit or be able to improve their performance might be correct; however, when it comes to improving performance, a "gut feel" isn't enough to justify introducing a performance improvement plan.

By using this method to measure their performance, we shift our discussions with employees on their performance from: "here is what I think of your performance" to "here are my observations on your performance, does this sound right to you?" The former suggests judgment and can often open debate, whereas the latter puts the onus on the employee to prove otherwise.

When someone's performance is below the level that is acceptable to you, using a baseline coupled with examples as outlined above puts the onus on *them* to identify why their performance isn't up to par, which accomplishes three things that make your life considerably easier:

1. It eliminates any perception of a personal conflict or bias.
2. It creates a dialogue and, in turn, a collaboration around individual development.
3. It solicits evidence-based feedback on how to improve performance.

By isolating low or poor performance in this manner, you remove the effort required to develop an individual on your team and transfer the ownership of such to that employee.

Our goal is to build a team in which we capitalize on top performers' strengths, improve the performance of mid-level performers, and either improve or replace those at the lowest levels of performance. Before you start handing out termination letters to your lowest-performing team members, let's discuss how to build this kind of structure (this is a joke, by the way!).

## GOOD, BETTER, BEST: A STRUCTURE FOR SALES TEAM GROWTH

In the movie Talladega Nights: The Ballad of Ricky Bobby,[8] Will Ferrell, who plays the role of Ricky Bobby, is famously known for the line "if you're not first, you're last." During a scene in the movie, Ricky's father, played by Gary Cole, visits Ricky during a career day at his school. He gets kicked out of the school for smoking in the classroom, and as he drives away, with Ricky and his classmates watching, he says, "Don't *listen to these people, Ricky. You're a winner. You got the gift. Always remember, if you ain't first, you're last.*"

Throughout the rest of the movie, Ricky focuses on winning every NASCAR race he enters until it ruins him, causing him to crash and lose his wife, car, and sponsors. Later in the movie, Ricky confronts his father and says, "Wait, Dad. Don't you remember when you told me, If you ain't first, you're last?" His father laughs off the memory and responds, "That doesn't make any sense at all. You're first or last. You can be second; you can be third or fourth. Hell, you can even be fifth.

This passage from the movie highlights a significant gap in how we tend to measure the performance of our sales team. When it comes to races or any competitive sport, we typically think about winning on multiple levels, not the first or last outcome. If, for example, you "podium" during a race, you are in first, second, or third place, all of which will get you a trophy and possibly some prize money.

When measuring our sales team's performance, many of the CEOs and Sales Executives I meet tend to think in terms of "*if you ain't first, you're last.*" Although this mindset might make measuring of the sales team's performance easy, it does little to recognize the skills and capabilities of the individuals within the team.

It's the same reason why, throughout school, there are multiple grades or percentage ranges to score a student's performance. The most common is a letter grade, with each letter representing where the student is performance-wise, as compared to the teacher's expectations and the performance of the rest of the class. These grades or ranges combine with comments that teachers can (and should) provide, give examples of strengths and opportunities for improvement and next steps.

When measuring performance, remember our goal is to accommodate differences in experiences, skills, and learning ability, all while motivating the employee to improve their performance rather than pushing them to win at all costs.

If you struggle with multiple performance levels, reflect on my earlier point about Ricky Bobby. He sought to win at all costs using the "if you ain't first, you're last" mentality. In the real world, if you can't achieve the level of performance set by your boss, you're likely to move in one of two directions:

1. You'll start to resent your boss for their inflexibility in measuring your performance and recognizing your strengths and shortfalls.

2. You'll leave the company, seeking a boss (and company) that offers more flexibility in how your performance is measured (and you are, in turn, rewarded).

Consider individual performance on multiple levels, like what you would experience in grade school. I call this the Good, Better, Best approach to measuring performance and you can apply it as follows:

## SHAWN'S GOOD, BETTER, BEST APPROACH TO MEASURING PERFORMANCE

### Basic Skill Level (Good)

Their efforts' results are acceptable and further development of skills and experience will result in improved or increased outcomes.

### Intermediate Skill Level (Better)

Results of efforts are better than an acceptable level. Developing and applying some new skills while improving existing skills will improve results.

### Advanced Skill Level (Best)

Results of efforts are at the highest level of performance. The skills and their application are completed at an advanced level, making this individual ideal to train, mentor, or coach others.

The key to using this approach to measuring performance is to set clear and specific steps, criteria, and results necessary to progress to the next level. Our goal is not to critique the individual but rather entice them to improve their performance.

The only way to do this effectively is to:

1. Give them the steps required to progress.
2. Identify the results achieved by completing them.
3. Provide examples of others who have achieved this.

Doing so bridges the performance gap and provides tangible steps for the individual to take to progress.

## ACCELERATING PERFORMANCE FROM BETTER TO BEST

Performance measurement can be highly subjective by nature. When I was teaching my boys to skate for the first time at the age of four and five, it began with having them watch me skate at a local arena. After seeing me in action for a few times (i.e., I'm not a professional skater, but I play on TV), they became eager to "join Daddy" on the ice. We then progressed to taking them out on the ice just to stand in one place and be surrounded by others skating (you've likely seen children in the center of an ice rink holding a chair or parent just watching others circle them). Once exposed in this way, the boys became interested in attempting to move on the ice (i.e., skate) and started working at building the skill. On the ice, having them apply what they had witnessed by moving their feet became the bridge between watching and doing.

Accelerating performance should be handled in the same way, namely:

- Observe others applying the skill (learning environment)
- Test application of the skill (experiential learning)
- Receive coaching on how to adopt and improve the skill (coaching and feedback)

Figure 5.2 outlines these stages.

Developing new skills among your "Better" team members is something your sales team have the natural desire to do, they just haven't yet had the opportunity to focus or unlock "how" to do so. This said, it's important to note that you can't force someone to improve their skills unless they believe there's a benefit they'll achieve as a result. Moreover, the perception of benefits will differ for each individual person on your team. In psychology, this is called Expectancy Theory,[9] originally presented by Victor Vroom,[10] a professor at the Yale School of Management. Victor's theory is that every individual will act or behave in a certain way as motivated to select a behavior on account of the expected outcomes. Further, the cognitive process for how each processes the motivational elements can differ.

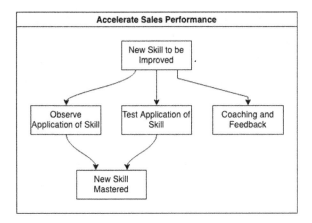

**FIGURE 5.2**
Accelerating sales performance.

For our purposes, know that what you personally find motivating may not motivate those on your sales team. Therefore, as sales leaders, we need to ensure that any rewards or recognition meet the following five criteria:

1. They are desirable by the individual.
2. They are desirable by most of our sales team.
3. They relate directly to performance.
4. The performance is reasonably achievable.
5. There are other options for those who don't find the rewards desirable.

For example, as a father of two boys heavily involved in sports, having the ability to take a Friday or Monday off to travel to and from hockey or baseball tournaments is something that is desirable. On the other hand, someone who doesn't have children may not find this as desirable.

*Accelerating* the development and application of new skills through recognition and rewards (while minimizing the time and effort on your part to assess the individual desirability for every member of your sales team) might seem overwhelming. It doesn't have to be however if you take the following steps:

**Sales Performance Acceleration Steps:**

1. Set clear targets for sales on both team and individual levels.
2. Explain how targets connect with and support the company's growth strategy.

3. Solicit ideas from your sales team on the rewards and bonuses they would find enticing.
4. Have team members identify their targets (considering past performance).
5. Have team members identify their rewards to achieve their targets.
6. Have all team members share their "ideal" plans with the entire team.
7. Facilitate a team discussion on what skills, resources, and tools are required to meet objectives.
8. Allow team members to adjust or update plans based on others' goals.
9. Review and finalize individual plans, validating targets and rewards.
10. Discuss with each individual and confirm the required support, skills, and resources.
11. Roll up individual development targets into your sales team performance plan.
12. Execute the plan, managing the performance of each closely.

## STORIES FROM THE SALES FLOOR

I was working with a team of salespeople, helping them to introduce new and more effective systems for selling, following my Unstoppable Sales$^{SM}$ framework. When it came time to create development plans, we discussed skills gaps the team perceived needed to be addressed, to assist them in accelerating their sales results. Each team member created their development plan, along with success measures to monitor their progress.

One of the team members, always eager to please, outlined several new activities he was going to introduce, following our work together. One of his goals was to book consistent meetings every week with new prospects. When I followed up with him a couple of weeks later, he hadn't made progress setting any new meetings, as he was "too busy helping his existing customers and dealing with inbound leads." This cycle continued over the next 4 weeks.

Recognizing the trend, I asked the Vice President of Sales to reach out and set a personal challenge for this individual, along with several others on the team. She reached out at the beginning of the following week and set a challenge of booking 10 meetings in the current week. The salesperson, always eager to please, had the meetings all booked within 48 hours.

Identifying and learning new skills that will improve our performance is sometimes the easy part. It's the application of the skills, which will achieve new results, that can be more difficult. By using a series of extrinsic and intrinsic motivators, you can ensure that everyone on your team has the willingness and ability to execute to achieve their performance targets.

The key to accelerating performance then is to create a development plan for every individual on the team, with their participation, suggesting the initial support they need, continuing with an open dialogue as they progress to address any gaps, needs, or wants.

By having the team members involved in the creation of their own development and performance plans, you create a more competitive environment that is self-motivated. Remember what we said at the beginning of this chapter, motivation is individual so what motivates you does not necessarily motivate everyone else on your sales team.

### UNSTOPPABLE SALES TEAM ACTION STEPS:

1. What performance baseline criteria matter most to your sales team?
2. Complete the Good, Better, Best categories for your existing sales team.
3. What strategies will you use to progress those in the "Better" category to "Best"?
4. What Performance Acceleration strategies will you use to further accelerate team and individual performance?

For a copy of my Sales Performance Acceleration Template to use with your sales team, see www.unstoppablesales.team

Next, let's discuss the essential skills you'll need to ensure your sales team adopts to sell in today's market.

# 6

## *The Top Sales Skills of an Unstoppable Sales Team*

There is no failure except failure to serve one's purpose.

**Henry Ford**
*Ford Motor Company*

With a performance baseline in place, it's time to turn our attention to the skills necessary to build (and accelerate) your sales team's performance. Fortunately, the list of skills a high-performing sales team needs to be effective is short. We'll discuss these shortly; however, first, let's look at one of the most overlooked criteria when adding new members to your sales team.

## WHY FIT IS MORE IMPORTANT THAN EXPERIENCE

A client of mine had hired a new team member for their sales team. The individual came with a laundry list of contacts, all of whom would be great contacts to sell their equipment. In addition, he had a background in sales, had worked in the mining industry for most of his career, and came with several rather glowing references from previous employers.

The first few months went well as the new hire began contacting his network, working the phones, and sending emails diligently. Next, he jumped into using the relatively new CRM software the company had purchased and set up workflows.

Beyond his sales performance, he participated in sales and other internal meetings and always showed up for work on time. On paper, he was

DOI: 10.4324/9781003348610-8

a great addition to the sales team, but something was amiss. The other members of the sales team didn't enjoy working with him.

During his time, he made several enemies, even outside of the sales department. For one thing, he constantly told his teammates what they should be doing, offering unsolicited advice, especially in front of the sales manager. In addition, he was overly demanding of those who influenced his ability to sell, constantly demanding improved lead times from Production and better payment terms from Finance. He even went so far as to set up tasks and assignments for his team members in their CRM software, often without advising them when doing so, then criticizing their inability to complete the tasks.

Six months in and the company let him go. In speaking with the sales manager, I asked, what about John led you to terminate his employment? "Well, for one thing, he hadn't sold anything, but it was more than that," she said. "John just rubbed everyone the wrong way, and although our clients and prospects seemed to like him, no one else did."

When it comes to building an unstoppable sales team, individual fit, within the sales team and the organization in general, is more important than skills. In my book, *The Unstoppable Organization*,[11] I spoke extensively about the importance of hiring for fit rather than experience, but for our purposes, here are the primary reasons:

- Selling is a team sport and requires collaborating with and engaging several internal departments (I call this *Making the Inside Sale*).
- Much of the motivation and inspiration for sales professionals come from close relationships with their peers and co-workers.
- Skills, including sales skills, can be taught, whereas fit within a team and an organization cannot. You either get along with those you work with or don't. You can't force fit within a team.
- The strongest sales teams consist of mentoring relationships, where senior sales representatives mentor those that are new to the team. Unfortunately, when there is a lack of trust or respect, mentoring is ineffective.

Simply put, you can't force a square peg into a round hole. For this reason, when you hire a new team member for your sales team, be vigilant in asking questions and assessing how well the team member will fit into your team. *Tip: involve members of your team throughout the hiring process to gain their insights and perspectives on how well the team member will fit.*

Let's also address those of you that might be thinking, "well, Shawn, if I hire a top performer, even if they don't fit amongst my team, their performance will naturally motivate the others to sell more." In the short term, I'd agree with you. However, it won't take long before resentment sets in, and suddenly your team members won't care about what your new super sales star achieves.

Hold on though, it gets worse. When you as a leader support, encourage, or get excited about the success of a team member who isn't a good fit, it diminishes trust the team has in you, as you are supporting someone they don't believe is a good fit for the team.

### STORIES FROM THE SALES FLOOR

Early in my sales career, I worked in a small sales team of four people, in addition to our sales manager. Two of the senior members were quite successful, and as a newer member of the team, I spent a considerable time asking them questions and observing how they interacted with prospects. There were also two junior sales reps, although I was the last to be hired.

Although we came from different backgrounds and had different levels of experience, we worked well together, covering each other during absences, shared lessons learned, and even shared prospects to help each other out during our day's off. Our sales supervisor was not overly demanding and periodically encouraged us to work together, which made it a good environment to work in.

Then the company owner hired a new salesperson who he introduced to everyone for the first time, *including the sales manager*. The new team member, Jim, seemed to check all the boxes of a great addition to the team, having worked in the industry for years, and seemed friendly and genuinely excited to work together. This didn't last. Within a week, Jim began making demands of the other team members. He was extremely protective of his prospects, warning the rest of us to stay away from anyone he talked too, then jumping at every prospect that showed up, rather than waiting his turn. It didn't take more than a few weeks before the rest of us disliked Jim. Within a few months, two of the newest team members had left, and within 6 months, the sales supervisor left, clearly irritated with the situation.

The wrong team member led to the dismantling of our very successful and somewhat collaborative sales team, all because the owner failed to recognize that fit within the team is more important than skills and experience.

## SEVEN CRITERIA FOR BEST FIT SALES TEAM MEMBERS

There's a chance you've jumped to this section of the book quickly. After all, if you have a sales team in place today, you may be eager to understand how to find and hire the "best fit" candidates for your sales team. If this is the case, make sure you go back to review the earlier chapters as they lay a foundation for assessing and building a foundation for your unstoppable sales team (Figure 6.1).

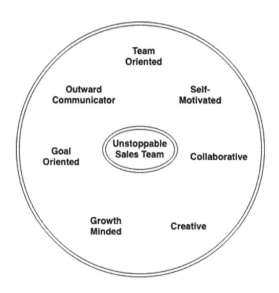

**FIGURE 6.1**
The seven elements of an unstoppable sales team.

If there's one thing I've noticed after working with hundreds of sales teams globally, it's that we tend to oversimplify the criteria of a good hire for our sales team, selecting team members who may be strong in some areas but extremely weak in orders. For example, many of the Sales Executives I work with will hire a superstar sales professional, who essentially have "sold them" on how great they are, only to find out later that they are a lone wolf with no interest in participating in or contributing to the betterment of the team.

A superstar sales professional is only worth their weight in gold if (and only if) they support your desire to improve the skills of the *entire sales team*. Without this willingness to share and support the broader team, any short-term sales they bring will erode the team's performance and results over time.

Instead, hire with the intention of finding someone who can help improve the skills and abilities of your existing team. Here, then are seven criteria to use when assessing and finding "right fit" candidates to join your sales team.

## SHAWN'S CRITERIA FOR HIRING NEW SALES TEAM MEMBERS

### Element #1: Team Oriented

The strength of a sales team results when the desire for personal growth and success is as strong individually as it is for the team. To be clear, being team-oriented is not the same as being a "team player." A team player gets along with and works well with their team members. Team-oriented is the view that the team's success is critical to individual success. They recognize that it may require additional effort to support their team, so they are willing to invest this time for the group's betterment. Peyton Manning[12] is an excellent example of someone who is team-oriented. Much of his success has resulted from his ability to bring two completely different teams to the Super Bowl. First, he helped get the Colts to the Super Bowl not once but twice during his 11 years as their quarterback. Then, after being traded to the Broncos, Peyton brought them to the Super Bowl twice during his 4 years as their quarterback.

### Element #2: Self-Motivated

This next element may seem counterintuitive. However, being team-oriented does not and should not detract from a salesperson's ability to be and remain self-motivated. Sales can be challenging, with constant rejection and a never-ending need to prove your worth. For this reason, top sales professionals need to be self-motivated, remaining optimistic and focused, despite the trials and tribulations they might experience.

We'll discuss motivation further in Chapter 8. For now, when hiring or selecting new team members, take the time to understand what drives them to maintain (or pursue) a career in sales. You can also spend time understanding other interests they may have and their reasoning for pursuing these interests. For example, I've been training at gyms since the age of fourteen. My reasons for doing so have evolved from not wanting to be the skinny kid in high school, to wanting to be fit to appeal to my future wife (lol), and today it's to remain healthy and increase my life expectancy. The reasons for my motivation have evolved, but it is their existence that keeps me going back to the gym several times each week.

When you find someone who is driven by their internal goals and needs, you'll find someone who is self-motivated and who will remain focused despite the varying obstacles and challenges they'll face.

### Element #3: Collaborative

When you are around those who are self-motivated, there is a natural tendency to be drawn to them, most often with the desire to learn from them. This learning results when we collaborate and can include soliciting the views and perspectives of other's during discussions, sharing ideas, and supporting each other in achieving goals or targets.

In sales, having the ability to collaborate is critical to a team's success. Collaboration will support your goal of building a learning environment among your team, as well as build more effective relationships with external departments, for example:

1. Collaboration with customer service to meet our customer's expectations.

2. Collaboration with production or operations to ensure the solution provided for the customer or client is what they desire.
3. Collaboration with Finance to ensure payment terms align with the customer's expectations.

If you want to select members for your team that will help you create an environment of Unstoppable Sales[SM], select those who are willing and able to collaborate effectively.

## Element #4: Creative

> Creativity is seeing what others see and thinking what no one else ever thought.
>
> **Albert Einstein**[13]

In sales, you're going to encounter a wide array of situations and circumstances. These might include a prospect that is near impossible to reach, a weird request, or even an objection never before heard (i.e., a prospect once told me they didn't want to meet with me as I brought too many ideas to the table and they couldn't handle any more priorities … I convinced him otherwise and his sales grew as a result).

We've all experienced these types of situations in which we weren't immediately sure how to respond. After test-driving a Pontiac Sunfire[14] (a compact car popular in the early 2000s), a prospect decided it wouldn't be a good car to buy because her cat needed more room on the backseat during their drives. There was the buyer I encountered who, after hearing pricing on our metal products, suggested that our price was too low to consider and likely meant poor quality.

Every sales professional will encounter unusual questions, objections, and situations during their career, and the degree to which you can overcome or move past these situations will determine your long-term success in sales.

Creativity is the ability to make or otherwise bring into existence something new, whether a unique solution to a problem, a new method, or device,[15] and is the skill that will determine the degree to which any sales professional will be successful.

When seeking new team members, share situations and examples that require them to demonstrate their ability to be creative.

## Element #5: Growth Minded

In her book, *Mindset, the New Psychology of Success*,[16] author Carol Dweck, Ph.D., discusses how there are predominantly two mindsets that anyone person can have. Someone with a growth mindset tends to view intelligence, abilities, and talents as skills that are learnable and can be improved upon with effort. Alternatively, someone with a fixed mindset views those traits as stable or fixed and unchangeable over time. A fixed mindset is close-minded to attempting to learn or apply new skills and often describes others' skills or abilities that are beyond theirs as "natural talent" rather than acknowledging the work and effort it took to reach their level of success in these areas.

When searching for new team members, spend time determining whether the individuals you are speaking to have a fixed mindset or a growth mindset. Look closely at their past experience and whether they've continued their "education" and skills building throughout their career.

## Element #6: Goal Oriented

The best sales leaders set targets for their sales team. These are most often in revenue; however, they can also include sales activities such as the number of contracts closed, the number of units sold, or even the value of orders closed. There is one problem; however, these goals are often individually motivating and can usually pull the team apart rather than bring them together. For example, being driven to achieve an individual revenue goal might result in pursuing leads that are better suited for my peers.

Focus on hiring sales professionals who are not only individually motivated by the pursuit of goals but also want to help others achieve their goals. The key is to set both individual and team goals, providing compensation and rewards for the achievement of both.

For example, when asked about hitting their monthly targets, do they stop once they meet their target or invest time in helping the team?

## Element #7: Outward Communicator

There is a difference between talking and communicating. The former is something that most sales professionals have mastered. The latter, not so much. For a sales team to be effective, there must be good communication

**FIGURE 6.2**
Top-down, bottom-up, and side-to-side communication.

from the top down and bottom up. So leadership must communicate effectively with all team members to ensure they can be successful, and those team members must communicate effectively with each other.

When communication is vital, both top-down and bottom-up, it creates an environment in which:

- Expectations are clearly understood and adopted.
- Coaching for improved performance is an accepted method.
- Feedback is welcomed and supports accelerated learning from past experiences.
- Concerns or frustrations are dealt with openly and promptly.

When you have good communication among team members, you create an environment where they learn from their leader and each other, which is a foundational element of building your unstoppable sales team (Figure 6.2).

## HOW TO ADDRESS MISTAKES AND ERRORS MADE BY YOUR SALES TEAM

As we discussed earlier in the book, the key to an unstoppable sales team is in creating an environment in which mistakes or errors are acknowledged and used as learning opportunities. Doing so allows you to rapidly escalate performance by avoiding mistakes and errors being repeated, all while creating an environment where the team is willing to test and trial new methods and ideas..

By my calculation, I've watched my son, who is thirteen at the time of this writing, play in over 144 baseball games. He is constantly practicing pitching, watching our local Blue Jays baseball team win (or lose) a game, and monitoring the stats of his favorite players across the MLB. Having grown up playing a bit of baseball myself, I enjoy the game, but he takes it to an entirely new level.

No matter how many games I watch, watching him make an error is always difficult; sometimes it's a ground ball that bounces over his head, or a pop-fly that falls short due to the sun in his eyes. In baseball, as in any sport, errors are common. Leading an unstoppable sales team comes with similar challenges:

> There will be mistakes and errors, and the ball will occasionally get dropped.

Whether you are leading a baseball team or a sales team, it's not a matter of if there'll be errors made but rather when those errors will happen. Here's the good news, though. Mistakes, errors, and mishaps are an opportunity to learn if they are shared openly with others. The key is creating an environment where mistakes are okay and lessons learned are shared publicly and regularly.

In my book *The Unstoppable Sales Machine*, I shared a proven strategy for opening up regular dialogue to enable the sales team to learn and share by having what I now refer to as a Daily Sales Huddle or DSH for short. DSHs are a standing-room-only, 20-minute morning brief in which the sales leader provides any updates, new information, or updates to the sales team, followed by an "around the circle" shared by team members for anything they want to share with the rest of the group.

## YOUR DAILY SALES HUDDLE

The key to achieving success through your DSH is by keeping the discussion brief, allowing you to maintain a standing-room-only approach, retaining people's attention, and ensuring the meeting keeps moving.

Depending on the size of your team, your DSH may only last 10 minutes, or it could extend to 30. After 30 minutes, however, I find people's attention spans wane, so keep it punchy and moving. If someone is going long on their comments or examples, ask them to share further information after the meeting via email or other methods.

When you introduce DSHs into your team's routine, it provides several benefits, including:

1. This a chance for you, as the sales leader, to share any important information or updates with the team.
2. A chance for the team to learn from one another by sharing errors, mistakes, or lessons discovered.
3. An opportunity for the team to collaborate.

For our purposes, let's focus on number two, the opportunity to share any mistakes, mishaps, or errors openly.

Keep in mind the DSH is brief, not intended to be long, drawn-out discussions or a time to explore *how* to resolve an issue but rather a quick share among team members to assist with learning and to avoid duplication of mistakes.

Here are some examples to share during your morning DSH:

- A team member made a mistake on a quote or proposal
- A quote or proposal was rejected due to an error
- A new buyer objection was overcome
- A meeting was missed, ran long, or ran short
- An opportunity to upsell or increase fees should have been noticed
- A buyer responded negatively toward a new approach or method
- A step should have been included in the sales process
- A sale was lost to a competition
- A deal was lost and feedback on the deciding factor was collected

To get started with introducing a DSH with your sales team, use the following format for your agenda and share it with the sales team to ensure they are prepared to participate:

1. Briefly describe the problem, mistake, or error encountered.
2. Why did this occur?

3. What was the impact?

4. How will you avoid the issue moving forward?

Building a strong sales culture is only possible if you, the sales leader, embrace and demonstrate it yourself. Despite your role, you must share your mistakes openly, acknowledging what you are changing and what you learned. For example, as a leader of an unstoppable sales team, you need to:

- Demonstrate your own errors.
- Ask questions to prompt your team to consider alternatives or solutions.
- Ensure prompt sharing of wins, mistakes, or losses among the team.
- Encourage open discussion and dialogue.
- Thank those who share their challenges to encourage others to do the same.

When you embrace the elements above, encouraging the sharing of mistakes and errors, you, in turn, create a sales team that is self-developing. The team learns when each member learns and having the elements in place for your decisions on who joins the team and how each member contributes and behaves creates an unstoppable force for selling.

There is more to leading an unstoppable sales team than embracing these elements and holding a DSH. So let's look at the activities, tools, and approaches you'll need to use to continue to build an unstoppable sales team next.

### UNSTOPPABLE SALES TEAM ACTION STEPS:

1. When would be an ideal time to introduce your own DSH?
2. How will you introduce the concept to your team and educate them on the agenda?
3. Who can help you champion the DSH to gain initial momentum?
4. What can you share openly during the DSH demonstrating your own vulnerability?

For a copy of your Daily Sales Huddle launch plan, see www.unstoppable sales.team

# 7

## *Creating an Environment That Stimulates Sales Team Performance*

You are a product of your environment. So choose the environment that will best develop you toward your objective ... Are the things around you helping you toward success—or are they holding you back?

**W. Clement Stone**
*American Businessman*

Selling is a multi-disciplined activity and in my experience working with sales teams globally, I've never met a top sales performer or a high-performing sales team that didn't have room to improve. This improvement, however, takes time, so painting a compelling vision of what the future looks like, for the individual, the sales team, and the organization as a whole, is key to ensuring your team members believe they have the runway to improve and experience the benefits of doing so.

## SETTING AND SELLING A COMPELLING FUTURE

In one of my previous sales jobs selling metal components, the Vice President (VP) of Sales was what I refer to as a target chaser. We met each week to review our sales targets individually with the VP and as a sales team. Every week he would run through a series of charts and graphs, contrasting our sales revenue against that of our targets. However, he never shared with us what the end state of all of our efforts was. Connecting the

DOI: 10.4324/9781003348610-9

numbers with where the company was heading and what benefit it would be to us to ensure it reached this point were mysteries to everyone.

When I was selling cars for a living, my sales manager drew the number of vehicles each salesperson was to sell on a whiteboard behind his door. My target was to sell 15 cars, so next to my name was 15 little car outlines, colored in as I made a sale. Next to small talk about the weather and our time off, the sales manager only asked one question about the sales teams work, "how many cars did you sell today?" If anyone sold a vehicle, they'd get a hearty "congratulations!" but if you'd sold none, he'd say, "There's still time in the day!"

In both situations, these were good managers and generally good people. They were easy to work with, friendly, and had the desire to help. Although I enjoyed working for them both, I left both jobs within the first 12 months, because the future, and my role within it, was unclear. Their hyper-focus on the near-term numbers (and results) painted a short-term picture for my career with them and their company.

As a sales leader, you create a short-term focus for your sales team when you focus only on the numbers and hitting near-term goals. Instead, we need to paint a crystal-clear picture of the future, which will engage our sales team to strive to achieve that future continuously.

The key to painting a compelling vision of the future for your sales team is to start with the destination in mind.

If I were to ask you, for example, to visit customers in Atlanta, Georgia, another one in Jacksonville, Florida, and then the third one in Phoenix, Arizona, the route you take would depend on two things:

1. Where you begin your travels.
2. Your desired destination upon completion of your travels.

You'll agree that with these two components, it is possible to determine what actions we need to take, the energy level to place into those activities, and what other support is required to succeed if we know our destination. In other words, our goal is what informs our actions.

Leaders of unstoppable sales teams paint a vivid picture of where their team is going. Their vision extends beyond providing weekly, monthly, or annual sales targets and addresses the more significant questions sales professionals ask themselves, namely:

- What are we trying to achieve as a team?
- What is the benefit to me to help us get there?

- What role can I play to help us get to our destination?
- How will you help me reach the goal?
- What will we get once we reach the goal?
- How will I be rewarded for my efforts?

The goal of these questions is to evoke a picture in the minds of our sales team as to what they are working toward, why it's essential, and what the benefit will be when we reach the destination.

Creating a compelling vision of the future and how it will benefit each of your team members may seem a bit daunting. Particularly, if your organization needs a clear vision or your sales team is so small that setting some grand vision of the future seems unnecessary. However, if you don't paint a picture of what the future looks like, employees will paint their own, which may involve working elsewhere.

## SHAWN'S STEPS TO CREATE A COMPELLING FUTURE

One of the first steps I take with any sales team on their journey toward being unstoppable is to assist them in creating their vision. The steps to creating your team vision are as follows:

1. Identify the company's vision for itself, its products, or its services. Consider areas such as:
   - Brand
   - Reputation
   - Market Position
2. Brainstorm the attributes the sales team would need to display to achieve this vision:
   - What role do sales play in achieving this vision?
   - How would we interact with the market?
   - How would our clients or customers describe us?
   - What would we have to do or not do?
3. Describe the outcomes of our attributes and connect them with the organizational vision.
   - How would our customers or clients describe us if we played our role well?

| Setting a Compelling Future for Your Sales Team | |
|---|---|
| Company Vision | Describe the brand, reputation, and market position you're seeking. |
| Sales Team Attributes | Sales team attributes to achieve this desired vision. |
| Attribute Outcomes | Outcomes of these attributes as they impact our customers and competition. |

**FIGURE 7.1**
Setting and selling a compelling future.

- How would our competition, prospects, and suppliers describe us?
- If we interact with clients in this manner, how would they describe their experience?

Use the following chart (Figure 7.1) to create a compelling future for your sales team.

With your compelling vision developed, let's move on to the next component necessary to stimulate high performance in your sales team, multi-directional communication.

## MULTI-DIRECTIONAL COMMUNICATION: PERSISTENT, PARALLEL, AND PERMEABLE

When building an unstoppable sales team, communication is the most powerful tool at your disposal. The key, however, is to be something other than the dominant communicator among the team, and instead invigorate communication among the team by focusing on encouraging parallel communication.

Recently, my oldest son was playing an exhibition game against another team in his league, and my wife and I were sitting near third base. Each time the other group went to bat, we could hear the third base coach instructing his team. There was a stark contrast between how the two different coaches, my son's coach and the coach on the other team, communicated.

Our coach was extremely quiet, and although he provided some coaching, he said very little. With the combination of a quiet voice and little instruction, it will come as no surprise that the cheering and chanting from my son's bench were also minimal at best. Alternatively, the coach from the other team was quite boisterous and chanted phrases that, to this day, I haven't heard from any other coach. For example, when a batter was up, he would say, in a voice that the entire team (despite where they were playing) could hear:

"Alright now, kid, be our Leader."
"Come on, let's do something cool."
"You got this, kid."

If a batter swung and missed, he yelled, "So What!" and if a batter struck out, he'd shout to his bench, "Guys, lift him up, don't let him walk back (to the dugout) alone."

Consider the stark contrast in communication between these two coaches, then consider the following question. Which team do you think was more energized and focused on the game? Was it our team's quiet coach or the other group's enthusiastic (and boisterous) coach? Moreover, which team do you think won the game?

Your sales team, like these coaches, will emulate your style and approach to communication. If you tend to be overly quiet, soft spoken, or outright rude when communicating with your team, they will be the same with you, the rest of the group, and in some situations, even with your clients or customers. For this reason, it's imperative that you consciously create and nurture the environment for how the team will communicate.

In an article titled "The New Science of Building Great Teams,"[17] Alex Pentland shared that their research had found that the most successful teams shared several defining characteristics. Specifically, everyone on the team talks and listens in roughly equal measure, team members connect directly with one another—not just with the team leader, and team members carry on back-channel or side conversations within the team.

The degree to which your environment will enable an unstoppable sales team is directly related to how effectively the team communicates. You choose the tone and agenda for this communication. Your goal must be to build communication using the 3 Ps as described below.

## SHAWN'S THREE Ps OF EFFECTIVE SALES TEAM COMMUNICATION

Persistent: set the tone for how your team communicates. Explain what information is to be shared, when to share it, and the best methods for doing so. Emulate this behavior yourself and be persistent with your expectations. The team will follow your lead.

Practical: the goal of any communication is to inform others. Keep communication functional and packed with helpful information the team can use and apply. For example, sharing the latest stock price only benefits the group if they are all investors. Alternatively, discussing new strategies to connect with busy buyers is practical and can be used immediately.

Permeable: for your team to be effective, they need the same information simultaneously. Practical information is only effective if it permeates the team. Side conversations or sharing information with part of the team serves to do nothing more than create a divide. For example, following team meetings, send a summary of critical points by email; when informal discussions break out among some team members, share the conversation with the broader team; if mistakes occur or new strategies identified, share them with the entire team.

By consistently practicing and applying the three Ps, you will create an environment that emulates Pertland's findings, providing a foundation for an unstoppable sales team. Building this kind of environment does take time. It begins with setting expectations around how you intend the team to communicate with each other. The value of doing so will provide in developing new skills to support more robust sales.

## ADOPTING A HUNGER FOR NEW SKILLS DEVELOPMENT

Daniel Greenberg once said, "You can't make someone learn something—you really can't teach someone something—they have to want to learn it. And if they want to learn, they will."

Our goal as the leader of an unstoppable sales team is to ensure our team wants to learn. So although you may create an environment ripe for learning as discussed earlier, we also need to create a compelling reason to participate in the learning environment. You can do so by focusing on three factors.

## FACTORS THAT INFLUENCE PARTICIPATION IN A LEARNING ENVIRONMENT

1. Mindset toward learning.

   As we discussed earlier, author Carol Dweck's book, *Mindset: The New Psychology of Success*,[18] discusses two different mindsets which underly beliefs toward learning and intelligence. Someone with a fixed mindset believes they have all the knowledge and intelligence they will ever have, whereas someone with a growth mindset continuously seeks new information to fuel their growth and learning.

   Someone with a growth mindset is open and eager for new learning; however, those with a fixed mindset are not. As leaders, our role is to help those with a fixed mindset transition to a growth mindset, which includes providing more optimistic language, encouraging failure as part of the learning process, and appreciating the learning process.

2. Purpose for learning.

   When a child is young and asked to do something, they consistently ask, "why?" For a period in their life, it's as if this is the only word in their vocabulary. The truth is our desire to understand why never changes; however, we learn, often through feedback from our parents, that we can't consistently ask why when faced with something new or different.

As leaders, we need to uncover the Purpose of every individual on our team. What drives them to come to work each day? What motivates them to work in the field of sales? Why do they work for our company over any other? By asking and uncovering the answers to these questions, we gain insights into what we will need to include as the reasons for participating in learning. For example, if your reason for working were to support your family, then position the value of learning as a means to gain new skills and earn more money to help your family.

3. Information absorption preferences.

In public school and into the early years of high school, I was what I would term an average student. My grades were typically all Cs, with the odd C+ for good measure. When forced to study for exams in high school, I realized my learning struggles resulted from my tendency to be a visual learner. Most of the teaching in those days resulted from sitting and listening to instruction.

How each individual on your team prefers to receive information will determine how much they desire to learn. For example, if you like to talk and explain everything, but your team members are visual learners, it is a little you'll share that they will retain, making the learning experience for both of you very frustrating. So instead, as leaders, we need to focus our time and energy on providing information for learning in three ways, namely:

Visual: providing images, displays, and diagrams
Audible: sharing steps, concepts, and resources verbally
Kinesthetic: incorporating hands-on learning to apply and practice new skills

When we apply all three of these learning methods to how our team members learn, we engage everyone in a way they'll find interesting, ensuring their engagement in the learning process and a faster path to applying new skills.

Although focusing on these three areas will create the right environment for learning individually, there are other factors that we, as leaders, need to practice to ensure learning new skills is exciting and deemed essential for development by the team.

## SHAWN'S RULES TO CREATE SALES TEAM ENGAGEMENT IN A LEARNING ENVIRONMENT

1. Reward mistakes. Members of our sales team should not fear reprimand or insults on account of making mistakes. Instead, recognize that mistakes are most often the result of trying new things, and as long as we learn from our mistakes, they are well-intentioned and valuable.

2. Encourage prudent risk-taking by team members. Stepping out of one's comfort zone, networking at a high-profile event, making cold calls, or even in presentations to game-changing prospects. When we encourage prudent risk-taking, we give our team members the approval to test and try new things.

3. Support self-development and deem it essential to any sales professional's career. I have invested over a quarter of a million dollars in coaching, training, and learning in the last decade alone. When we encourage self-development and create expectations around time invested in self-development, we shift the perspective many sales professionals have that learning takes time away from selling. Time away from selling can assist us with selling more effectively.

4. Encourage team problem-solving. Many sales leaders see themselves as needing all the answers, which, as you might imagine, is impossible. Instead, see yourself as having a network of people and resources that can assist in helping your team solve problems. Connect team members to explore issues and invite outside views and opinions to address common challenges. Use the reach of your network and your unique position of being able to put people together as your secret weapon in helping your team solve their problems.

5. Encourage multi-directional communication. As a sales team leader, effectiveness of communication can make or break your sales team's development. Our goal must be to encourage and facilitate communication from our team (bottom-up) and among our team (side-to-side). We should consistently communicate with the individuals on our team and the group as a whole. You are the conduit that drives information, lessons learned, new strategies, and best practices throughout the team. Use your power to facilitate these communications.

Sales meetings are one of the best means to facilitate communications among your sales team, building a culture that embraces and applies to learning. Unfortunately, many sales leaders need to be more effective at facilitating their sales meetings, which is why I've dedicated an entire section of this book to how you should be organizing, facilitating, and using your sales meetings to support your sales team.

## SALES MEETINGS THAT STIMULATE LEARNING

One of the most common and effective means of communication is through your sales meeting. These differ from the Daily Sales Huddles mentioned earlier and often are done on a weekly or monthly basis, bringing the sales team together to review results, introducing new products or services, and strategizing about growth opportunities. Although these meetings can come in various forms, they are often designed to suit the needs of the sales leader rather than the sales team.

There are three participants in any sales meeting, namely:

1. The Sales Leader
2. The Sales Professional (those among the team)
3. The Sales Team (comprised of several sales professionals)

These different groups each have varying objectives for the sales meeting, for example:

1. The sales leader wants to learn about any struggles or challenges the sales team faces hindering their ability to sell.
2. The sales team wants to know what's working for their peers to sell more.
3. The individual team member wants to understand how the company can assist them in selling more.

Most sales meetings are also run or facilitated by the Sales Leader, designed to address their needs and objectives rather than around the three groups mentioned above. They use the meeting to share product updates, discuss customer or client concerns, and request performance updates from their sales team. These are all necessary, but most often do nothing to serve the needs of the team members or the team. As a result, the sales meeting can be a painful and complete waste of time. You've never been in a meeting that was a waste of time, have you?

So, the obvious question, then, is how do you know if your sales meetings are hindering or helping the performance of your sales team? The most obvious signs are a lack of engagement or participation by the sales team and can also include complaints from your staff about the value of the meeting. Other examples can include any or all of the following:

- Participants show up late for the meeting without a good reason.
- Despite consistently attempting to engage the team, there needs to be more participation during the meeting.
- Participants are distracted during the meeting, checking emails or texts.
- You receive complaints about the meeting taking too long or that participants need more time to join.
- Body language that suggests a lack of interest, including slouching or rolling of eyes.

Here's the simplest measure. If you think your employees aren't interested in participating in your sales meeting, you're probably right.

To create a valuable sales meeting, start with an agenda and a format that enable the team's involvement, interest, learning, and engagement. There are three areas for you to consider as follows:

## SALES MEETING PREPARATION

For effective sales meetings, build the meeting and agenda around the three different groups by asking yourself the following questions:

1. What information is essential that I share at this meeting that is new and time-sensitive?
2. What information do my team members want to take away that will help them to sell more?
3. What information will be helpful to the entire sales team?

## SALES MEETING FORMAT

Create a format for the meeting that engages every participant. My recommendation is that, following your sharing of information (which should take no more than 20 minutes), go "around the room," asking each of the participants if they have any questions, concerns, or group shares that would be valuable to others.

Provide each participant 5 minutes for their share but remain flexible if the claim takes longer and the information is helpful to others. Manage those who tend to talk for the sake of talking by reinforcing the 5-minute rule. Additionally, if a participant has nothing to share, that's also okay. The objective is to ensure everyone can share something they deem necessary with others.

## SALES MEETING OUTCOMES

To capture key points raised or discussed, ask someone to take notes of important points raised during the meeting. You might select someone who enjoys taking notes, or my preference was to send these notes myself. The key is highlighting essential points from the meeting, not everything discussed. Send this to all participants post-meeting for reference and follow-up or further discussion if necessary.

In addition to the steps above, there are ten commandments to effective sales meetings you should adopt as follows:

**Shawn's Ten Commandments for Effective Sales Meetings:**

1. The meeting shall begin and end on time.
2. There shall be a clear agenda in advance of the meeting.
3. The agenda shall contain points that are interesting to the sales team.
4. The meeting shall open with an exciting and relevant announcement for the team.
5. Participants shall share wins and other successes at the beginning and end of the meeting.
6. Employees shall have roles that enable their participation in the meeting.

7. The sales leader shall not share negative comments or views during the meeting.
8. The meeting shall end with each team member having a chance to speak.
9. Actions arising from the meeting shall be clear, have a due date, and be assigned.
10. Actions noted during the meeting shall be shared in writing post-meeting.

For a printable version of the Ten Commandments for Effective Sales Meetings, visit www.unstoppablesales.team

The goal of any sales meeting is to create an environment in which the sales team, and the individuals within it, gain information that will assist them in selling more. It takes more than information, however, to achieve sales. Therefore, we need to stimulate the application of this information, and coaching is the best way.

### UNSTOPPABLE SALES TEAM ACTION STEPS:

1. How will you create a compelling vision for your sales team?
2. What methods can you introduce to increase the effectiveness of your communication?
3. How can you improve your sales meetings?
4. How are you applying the ten commandments in every one of your sales meetings?

With our environment ripe for learning and high performance, let's turn to one of the most powerful tools in your arsenal to prompt high performance. That's our next chapter.

# 8

## *Motivation Doesn't Come from Within*

People often say that motivation doesn't last. Well, neither does bathing – that's why we recommend it daily.

**Zig Ziglar**
*American Author and Motivational Speaker*

If you were to ask any sales leader today what motivates their sales team, the most common answer you'd receive is "money." It's why many sales leaders and their organizations offer commissions, bonuses, and various other forms of compensation. However, pinpointing the real sources of motivation for a sales team (and the people within it) is quite a bit more complex. Consider for example that the study of human motivation has been presented in various forms, from Hertzberg,[19] to Taylor.[20]

After nearly 15 years working with hundreds of sales teams, I've found Maslow's Hierarchy of Needs[21] to be the most suitable means of uncovering what motivates sales professionals to join a sales team, stick with that team, and strive for higher levels of performance. Figure 8.1 depicts Maslow's hierarchy as it pertains to what motivates today's sales professionals.

Maslow's findings are relevant for our purposes because they depict the individual relationship each of our team members has with motivation. Although we can always draw some reasonable assumptions on what motivates our employees (i.e., reassuring them of the security of their job), the degree to which a team member is motivated is something you need to assess individually.

For example, what it takes for me to feel "secure" in a job may be very different compared to your definition. As it pertains to income, the

DOI: 10.4324/9781003348610-10

**FIGURE 8.1**
The sales professional's hierarchy of needs.

amount of income that I believe is necessary for achieving "security" might be very different than yours. Additionally, the degree of importance you might place on belonging, fitting in with my co-workers, and appreciating my manager is likely to differ from other employees.

But we must look deeper to understand what motivates our team members. Think of it like peeling back an onion.

When you think about helping your team members feel "safe" or "secure," what are the areas in which you can have influence? Common examples that come to mind may include any or all of the following:

Compensation, including wages and bonuses.
Benefits and healthcare.
Retirement support, including 401K or RSP (Retirement Savings Plan) matching programs.
Feedback and support from a manager.
Feedback and support from company leadership.
Financial stability of the company.
Diversification of customers.
Privately owned versus publicly traded.
The type of product or service sold.
Diversification of products or services sold.
Size of the company (including the number of locations and employees).
Age of the company.
Location of the company.
Tenure of the employees.
Tenure of company ownership and leadership.

As sales leaders, our ability to motivate our team depends on how accurately we can identify the common motivators for the team, the individual motivations of each member of the team, and the degree of relevance these motivators have on individual team members.

Although motivation can be complex, it's relatively easy to manifest for your team once you understand the necessary ingredients. So don't let the complexity of motivating your team be daunting; however, do realize that motivation requires some effort on your part and isn't as simple as taking your team to lunch.

Although I speak at a wide variety of events and sales meetings annually to help "motivate" the sales team, I've never considered myself as a motivational speaker, but rather an invigorator of action. My job is to provoke and inspire the audience to grasp new ideas and put them into action. The motivation will result once they do and see the promised results.

Now, let's start to motivate your sales team.

## WHY MONEY IS NOT A MOTIVATOR: HERE IS WHAT IS

Early in my sales career, I worked for a Sales Director who believed money was the only motivator for his sales team. It was his default solution for any (and every) situation that arose such as:

- If sales slowed, he offered a cash bonus to the first person who could make a sale in a set period.
- If you reached a specific monthly sales target, he'd add a cash bonus to incentivize you to sell one more unit.
- If you worked every day without missing any time being sick during the year, he'd pay you a cash bonus at the end of the year.

For example, he would bring the entire sales team in to work on the Saturday of a long weekend despite requests to take the weekend off (and there had never been a new car sold on a long weekend during the company's history).

He pulled the team together first thing in the morning, offering a cash bonus at the end of the day for anyone that could make a sale. Naturally, the more senior members of the sales team rolled their eyes and returned to what they were doing, but being new, I was eager, so I eagerly began working the phones and reaching out to my list of prospects, doing everything I could to get at least one of them to come to the store.

Not surprisingly, being a long weekend, I didn't reach anyone (although many did come to the store the following week). Finally, during the last hour of the day, a young lady stopped by from out of town. We had met several weeks before; however, she had not demonstrated any interest for buying a car at the time. After some initial discussion, she shared that she had been looking at our competitors' products but had enjoyed our conversation and had returned, ready to make a purchase. Hallelujah! I thought. We created the order together and I took it to my team leader, who eagerly signed off. After a final discussion with my client, I walked into the manager's office with the deal, signed, sealed, and delivered. As I waited for the congratulations to begin, there was a long pause. After reviewing the agreement, the manager said, "I'm not selling at this price! You had better find a way to increase the price; otherwise, this deal isn't any good."

Shocked, I stood in silence, looking at the supervisor, who just shrugged. Although not as high a margin as some, this deal was still well within our regular margins. I returned to my client and discussed some options that would make her investment better (a paint coating with a lifetime warranty against fading and cracking), to which she agreed, and I returned to the manager's office with the updated deal.

He smiled and responded, "I knew you could do it, Shawn; great work! Let me get you the cash I promised. I took the cash home that day, and then took my talents elsewhere later that month. Although the cash bonus that day was a motivator, the manager's use of the so-called incentive wasn't.

When it comes to motivating your sales team, there are:

- Motivators you can directly influence (i.e., compensation, support from the manager).
- Motivators you can indirectly influence (i.e., diversification of customers, tenure of employees).
- Motivators you have no control over (i.e., company's location and age).

## Shawn's List of Sales Team Motivators

We've already looked at "Safety and Security" and the various ways members of your team may define what constitutes motivation, so let's look at the remaining aspects of Maslow's work. It's important to note that these may include motivation for individuals on your team, but as mentioned earlier, you'll need to identify which are most applicable individually.

1. **Belonging:** Examples of individual expectations around belonging can include:
   - Connection and relationships with members of the team.
   - Fellowship and relationship with your direct manager.
   - Relationships and interactions with other managers.
   - Relationships and interactions with senior leadership.
   - Relationships with co-workers.
   - Connection with customers.[22]

   Belonging summarized: if an employee's perception is that they are not a fit within the team, the organization, or with the kinds of prospects and customers you work with, they will not feel as if they belong, resulting in disengagement and ultimately either low performance, high turnover, or a combination of both.

2. **Esteem:** Examples of individual expectations around esteem can include:
   - Personal recognition needs.
   - Team recognition needs.
   - Leadership treats them and others with respect (as defined personally).
   - Prospects and customers treat them with respect (as defined personally).
   - Self-esteem needs are satisfied.
   - Freedom to behave and speak in a personally satisfying manner.

   Esteem summarized: if an employee's esteem needs, which are individually defined, are not met, it will directly impact their confidence and willingness to take on new assignments, pursue prospects, and close sales.

3. **Self-actualization:** Examples of individual expectations around self-actualization can include:
   - Encouraged to pursue skills development by their manager.

- Encouraged to seek skills development by the company and other leaders.
- Present opportunities to improve skills (aligning with individual needs).
- Requests for skills development are supported.
- Realization of new skills and talent.
- Recognition of changes in one's performance and perspective.

Self-Actualization summarized: similar to the other areas of Maslow's hierarchy, you'll notice that self-actualization is personally defined. Therefore, a sales leader who supports this area of motivation must be adept at recognizing the strengths of each person on their sales team and encouraging continued development that will assist everyone in growing both personally and professionally.

Recognizing how complex motivation can be, let's shift our focus to how you, as a sales leader, can directly influence and impact your team's motivation.

## SALES LEADER INFLUENCE OVER MOTIVATION

At this point, you might be wondering if you will ever be able to motivate anyone! Have no fear. Fortunately, there are four simple ways in which you can consistently motivate your sales team. Focusing your attention on these areas will drive your behavior to naturally recognize the individual influence motivation has on your team members.

### Influence Area #1: Awareness

When coaching sales leaders on increasing their team's motivation, I reinforce the importance of awareness. To improve our ability to motivate our team, we must first recognize the dichotomy between what inspires us and what motivates others. As we discussed at the beginning of this chapter, just because I may be motivated by frequent challenges that can reward me with additional monetary compensation doesn't mean the same holds for you.

To reflect on how best to motivate both the team and those members within the group, ask yourself a simple question, *"How can I best position this idea, initiative, or challenge in a way that team members will be motivated and embrace it?"* Reflecting on this simple question will drive you to consider everyone on the team, particularly those you find most challenging to motivate, considering ideas that might assist with how you best position this new idea or initiative.

For example, you want to motivate everyone to close a new deal within the next week. Providing an incentive such as a cash bonus or time off would seem appropriate but may only inspire some on your team.

A better answer results when we ask ourselves a better question, such as *"How can I best position this challenge so that team members will be motivated to embrace it?"*

Doing so will help you arrive at several additional options, such as one-to-one time with the CEO, recognition among the team or organization, celebratory lunch, etc. You will motivate more team members to achieve your objective by providing better choices or several options.

In essence, this question will force you to think more broadly about methods to motivate and drive you to consider what methods will be most embraced by the team.

## Influence Area #2: Positioning

No matter the value of the ideas, if you introduce them in a non-motivating way, most of your team will likely avoid embracing them. With plenty of ideas and strategies that you believe will motivate your team, considering how you'll position these ideas becomes the difference between whether the team will accept and adopt the views or dismiss them.

The positioning includes the following considerations:

- What is the benefit and value of agreeing to this?
- What language should be used to increase understanding and adoption?
- What possible objections or pushback might come when introduced?
- How will I address these objections in my presentation?
- How does this align or support other focus areas?

You'll want to consider how to position each motivational idea to ensure it will entice the team (and each individual on the team) to embrace and adopt it, becoming motivated in the process.

## Influence Area #3: Timing

As the saying goes, timing is everything. For example, it's unlikely you would write up a quote during an initial prospect meeting and request they sign it on the spot, and the same goes for sharing motivational strategies with your sales team. So be selective WHEN the best time is to share these ideas to ensure they land with the impact you expect.

Selecting your timing includes asking yourself the following questions:

- When is the best time to present this challenge or initiative?
- Are there other competing priorities or distractions that may limit its impact?
- How can I align this with our other existing priorities?
- What day and what time of day would be best to present this?
- When and how frequently will I re-affirm and reinforce this idea?

The goal here is not to paralyze you with analysis paralysis but instead choose your timing wisely. Then, when you have the best positioning and timing, your message will land with your sales team as if it is a natural progression or extension of other current priorities.

## Influence Area #4: Indirect Impacts

With each of the above areas considered, take stock of your indirect impacts on your team's motivation. Think of these as those things that may have your team question the validity of your idea or whether your intent (to motivate them) is genuine. For example, attempting to motivate your team to work harder with more prospecting activities during slow periods is acceptable; however, if you decide to take a vacation or leave work early during that period, it can send the wrong message. Likewise, raising your voice (or pounding your fist on the desk—which I've witnessed many sales leaders do) does nothing to motivate your team to embrace your ideas.

To avoid indirect impacts affecting your ability to motivate your team, consider the following:

- Do my behaviors reinforce and support the messages I've shared with the team?

- Am I acting in a way that reinforces the importance of what I've asked of the team?
- Does my demeanor or attitude align with the expectations I've placed on the team?
- Does my work ethic align with the expectations I've placed on the team?
- Do I always maintain my composure in difficult or stressful situations?
- Where my behavior doesn't align with what I expect of the team, am I transparent about why this is, and apologize for any unacceptable behaviors?

When you consider and apply these four areas of influence over your motivation, you'll ensure that your ideas, suggestions, and recommendations land with the impact you expect.

## STORIES FROM THE SALES FLOOR

Early in my sales career, I worked for a sales manager who, at least initially, seemed to be highly focused on motivating me, as well as the rest of the team. Several of us were hired at once, so our experience over the preceding weeks and month were nothing but positive. We had weekly meetings where new products were introduced, information was shared on upcoming promotions, and ideas were presented on how we could capitalize on marketing initiatives to generate the most sales. In addition to his very supportive attitude toward our success, he shared with us some virtual sales training that was meant to support us in hitting the ground running.

For all intents and purposes, I was excited for the role, the company, and to have him as my manager. Unfortunately, this feeling was short-lived.

It became clear very quickly that my sales manager was solely focused on our ability to hit our targets. It was as if he couldn't hold a conversation without first asking how we were doing as compared to our weekly and monthly targets.

One day, early in my career, I sheepishly asked for his help with a family looking for a product we didn't have. He sighed, arose from his desk and said "I'll show you how this is done Casemore," walking by me as he greeted the family and began presenting the product.

After closing the deal with the family, he turned to me and said "do you think you can you take it from here?" in a somewhat condescending voice. You won't be surprised to learn that he didn't count closing the deal toward my targets.

---

## MOTIVATING YOUR SALES TEAM: THE EVERYDAY SALES MANTRA

To begin with, consider that there are three kinds of memory every human being has, namely:

1. Short-term memory, which can last from seconds to hours (i.e., I need to pick up bananas at the grocery store).
2. Long-term memory, which can last a lifetime (i.e., my anniversary is 15 June).
3. Working memory allows us to retain information for a limited time (i.e., your phone number is 555-1212, 555-1212, 555-1212).

The efforts and initiatives you will introduce to motivate your team will initially land in their short-term memory. For example, a compliment you pay someone for a job well done, a coffee you buy for the team after they work late on a presentation, or a cash bonus you give after someone closes a deal.

In some instances, the impact your motivation has on an individual can land it in their long-term memory (i.e., the time you presented them with a meaningful award in front of the rest of the organization); however, most will be short-lived.

For our purposes here, and without diving into the psychology of human behavior, you can use some simple strategies to ensure the motivation you share has a long-term impact. To this point in the chapter, we've discussed various methods and focuses for motivating your sales team; however, many of these will take time to introduce and experience results.

Motivation is measured individually; although you may introduce something we've discussed today, it may take 6 months to a year or longer for everyone on the team to be fully motivated. So don't be discouraged;

I have something simple you can use starting today that will impact your team immediately.

One of the easiest ways to motivate your team is by repeating impactful statements regularly. This aids in cementing these ideas into the long-term memory of your team and, in turn, achieves what Zig Ziglar referred to at the start of this chapter on motivating your sales team daily. I call it the Everyday Sales Mantra, or ESM for short.

An ESM is an impact statement, slogan, or saying repeated frequently and with enough conviction and meaning that it will land in your sales team's long-term memory. To be clear, I'm not suggesting you have your team line up in front of the mirror each day to repeat something intended to motivate them. An ESM is a phrase that you repeat, as the leader, to reinforce the focus for your team, all to assist them in remaining motivated to move forward. Additionally, you can have more than one ESM that you use and ultimately will become known for, helping you to reinforce various essential messages that will motivate your team.

## YOUR EVERYDAY SALES MANTRA STRUCTURE

In this section, we will design your ESM and provide examples of when and how to apply it for the most significant impact. First, let's start with the structure.

Your ESM should be:

1. Brief and memorable.
2. Something your sales team can relate to.
3. Clear and avoid complex language.
4. Something others outside your sales team can understand.
5. Quickly recognized when you begin to repeat it.

Here are some examples of past ESMs I've used with sales teams as part of my training and work.

### Example ESM #1

*Remember the golden rule; we must practice the ABPs of selling—Always Be Prospecting.*

## Example ESM #2

*Focus on what you can control, not what you can't.*

## Example ESM #3

*Let's get out there and sell something.*

## Example ESM #4

*You decide how to best use your time, no one else.*

## Example ESM #5

*You can't control what your buyer will do; you can only control how you respond.*

You'll notice that these are simple and relatable statements. However, to help your team adopt your ESM, you must repeat it when the opportunity presents itself. When you do so, you create impact with the statement; that is, you tie it to something your sales team can relate to, which will move it from their short-term memory to their long-term memory.

I'll suggest you are already making repeated statements that have the ingredients for your ESM, so as a next step, let's develop your ESMs that you can use today. First, work through the following questions as your guide, noting your responses in the form of points or statements. Once complete, you will have the ingredients to formulate your own ESMs.

1. What are some of the frequent challenges your sales team presents to you?
2. What solutions can your team use or apply to overcome these challenges?
3. How do you typically respond to assist them in moving past these challenges?
4. Of these responses, how can you structure these into single statements or brief sentences?
5. Read these aloud or ask a peer to help you determine the most impactful ones.

## MEASURING THE SUCCESS AND IMPACT OF YOUR ESM

It's important to mention that your ESM will not solve your employee's challenges or concerns or replace your responsibility to support your sales team with their challenges. Instead, they become a predictable response complimented by your assistance, support, or encouragement. In other words, your ESM cannot be an empty statement to avoid supporting your team but rather a message you use while helping your team. The combination of your action and a verbal response creates the impact that results in motivation.

So, with your ESMs in hand, begin using them daily, making minor adjustments as you see their impact on the team. Continue to improve them over time until you have something you can repeat. The ultimate measure of the success of your ESM will be when your employees start saying them on their own. This confirms they are being retained in your team's long-term memory and begins the process of supporting their motivation.

Leading an unstoppable sales team requires more than your ability to motivate your team, so in Part 3, let's uncover the key attributes and practices you'll need to deploy if you genuinely want to build an unstoppable sales team.

### UNSTOPPABLE SALES TEAM ACTION STEPS:

1. What are some motivators that have been proven to work with your sales team today?
2. What other (new) motivators could you introduce?
3. What will your ESMs be?
4. How can you use your ESMs in a way that will support your sales teams motivation?

For a series of motivational questions you can use to help you reflect on steps to motivate your team and its members, see www.unstoppablesales. team

With your sales team now motivated, let's dive in deeper to discuss the methods and strategies you'll need to use to lead your team to unstoppable levels.

# Part III

# A Sales Leader's Guide to Managing an Unstoppable Sales Team

The pessimist complains about the wind. The optimist expects it to change. The leader adjusts the sails.

**John Maxwell**
*American author, and speaker*

Managing an unstoppable sales team requires a people-centric leader who places the development and success of their team over their own, encouraging everyone on the team to strive for new levels of performance.

If this doesn't sound like you, have no fear. After working to develop strong leaders for nearly 15 years, I can reassure you that strong leaders like this are built, not born. The key is that you can change how you think, act, and behave. It's not easy work, but it is rewarding.

In this chapter then, we'll discuss the critical aspects of leading an unstoppable sales team and the attributes and characteristics of a successful leader.

DOI: 10.4324/9781003348610-11

# 9

## *Your Role as the Leader of an Unstoppable Sales Team*

The difference between building your team to unstoppable levels and having a sales team that performs at average levels is determined by the type of leader you are. It takes a special kind of leader to have the desire, ability, and discipline to build and lead an unstoppable sales team, and for a good reason.

To be an effective leader is hard work, requiring that you consistently focus on both the individual needs and abilities of team members, as well as the success and wellness of the entire team as a unit. Essentially, you must prioritize each member's success while ensuring the team works together to achieve its objectives. As you strive to achieve this balance, you'll need to place the success of others before your own and put the entire team's success ahead of that of individuals who exist on the team. In other words, your sales team and its ultimate success is your top priority, above all else.

Figure 9.1 demonstrates the key focus areas for an unstoppable sales team leader.

If you're willing to put in the work to build a sales team that is unstoppable, your capability as a leader will determine how quickly you can build the team, how effective they will be, and the extent to which you can accelerate and sustain their new levels of performance. In other words, if you follow the steps I've laid out in building your team to this point and their performance levels have not improved, it's time to look in the mirror.

DOI: 10.4324/9781003348610-12

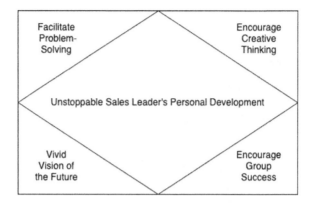

**FIGURE 9.1**
Key focus areas for an unstoppable sales leader.

## THE DIFFERENCE: REGULAR LEADERS VERSUS LEADERS OF UNSTOPPABLE SALES TEAMS

My father, now in his eighties, led a team of about ten staff for over 15 years until he retired. I recall as a teenager that for him, leading the team and still performing his job wasn't easy. When I was in my early twenties, I began leading my first team, and I recall sharing some of my frustrations with him. The real question for me at the time was, is being a manager and having all the responsibilities that come with "management" worth it? My father, then retired, laughed and said, *"well, Shawn, I can't tell you too many interesting stories about my accounting career, but I can certainly share plenty of interesting stories about the people I led and worked with."* His point is that leading others is some of the most rewarding work you'll do, despite its many challenges. Having led over a dozen different teams in various companies early in my career, I'd have to agree.

Over the years of working with and coaching a wide variety of sales leaders and executives globally, I have noticed that leaders of unstoppable sales teams possess unique attributes, setting them apart from typical sales leaders.

These leaders possess a high degree of emotional intelligence, which supports their focus on the betterment of the team; however, leaders of unstoppable sales teams also demonstrate and encourage the very attributes they seek in building their sales team, namely:

1. **Personal development:** they place a priority on the personal development of both members of the team and themselves. Team training, individual learning, and coaching are all tools they embrace to improve performance consistently.
2. **Have a vivid vision of the future:** they hold and share a vivid vision of the future, consistently engaging their team in the pursuit of the vision and answering the question, "what does our future look like?"
3. **They facilitate team problem-solving:** leaders of unstoppable sales teams don't solve problems; instead, they present problems and challenges to their team, assisting them in identifying possible solutions and next steps.
4. **They encourage creative thinking:** there are no bad ideas when leading an unstoppable team. Consistently encouraging new ideas and out-of-the-box thinking is a cornerstone of how these leaders interact with their teams.
5. **They encourage group success:** these leaders place the success of the team and individuals on the team ahead of their own. They don't pit team members against each other in competitions but instead set challenges that require the team to work together and achieve success.

While leading a team of 27 unionized staff earlier in my career, we faced a critical staff shortage. After we returned from Christmas vacation, two of my staff decided to retire early and a third transferred to a different division. So we had 2 weeks before all three team members were gone.

After speaking to my Vice President, a temporary employee named Tom transferred to my team as interim help until I could go through the long, drawn-out process of hiring through the union. I was excited as Tom had a reputation as a hard worker, and generally, everyone enjoyed working with him. On his first day on the job, we sat down, and I laid out Tom's role and what I would require of him as a team member and, of course, asked what support I could provide. Not one to mix words, Tom said, "Shawn, look, I'm just here temporarily to help out until you can hire more people, so how long do you think before I can get back to my other team?" Todd was uncomfortable with his new assignment. Not one to mislead anyone, I responded, "I'm not sure how long I'll need you, Tom, but I appreciate your willingness to help out."

Two years later, Tom was still working with our department and had become part of the fabric of the unstoppable team we had built. Tom tackled any challenge in front of him, worked well with others, and contributed to discussions and ideas on how we could continue to improve as a team. Around this time I was promoted and announced to my team that I'd be moving on, but only after I found a suitable replacement. Shortly after making the announcement to my team, I was walking by Tom's desk, and he stopped me. "Shawn," he said, "do you know why I never brought up being transferred back to my old department after our discussion that day a couple of years ago?"

"No," was my response, curiously waiting to hear why Tom had never brought this up again. "It's simple," he continued, "for years, I've worked for a variety of bosses, and you are the only one that ever listened to my concerns and then actually tried to do something about them." The look on my face must have reflected being flattered but a tad confused as Tom continued, "basically, you deal with all of the s*it I face so that I can just do my job."

The light bulb went on that day, and this example has stayed with me ever since. Above all else, leaders of unstoppable sales teams ensure that overcoming the issues, concerns, and barriers their team encounters as their top priority. Their team's success becomes their success.

Let me give you some simple examples of what you might encounter as a sales leader, and how you would respond as the leader of an unstoppable sales team:

**Example scenario #1:** An employee suggests that the CRM (Customer Relationship Management) system isn't logging calls when they try to use it for outbound calling. The leader of an unstoppable sales team makes it their priority to connect directly with IT or the CRM provider to resolve the problem.

**Example scenario #2:** An employee complains that they receive payment for their travel expenses well after paying the credit card bill. An unstoppable sales team leader immediately sits with HR (who wrote the policy) and Finance to devise a solution to more prompt payment.

**Example scenario #3:** Employees complain that leads provided by marketing or an external marketing firm need to be of better quality, and it's wasting much of their time to vet the leads. The leader of an unstoppable sales team will call a meeting with marketing to share examples and better understand how to improve the quality of the leads.

From each of these scenarios, you'll notice some distinct behaviors, namely:

1. The leader is involved in every situation directly; they don't put off or assign responsibility for resolving the issue to someone else (although they are likely to include others in finding the solution).
2. Their response is immediate. Of course, they'll first confirm that others are facing a similar issue, then take appropriate action to resolve the problem quickly. Their team's concerns, challenges, and barriers become their main priority.
3. They collaborate. In each situation, they work with other departments who may influence or create the challenge and seek a solution through collaboration. By doing so, they find an outcome that isn't a workaround but a sustained solution that everyone can accept.

If you want to lead an unstoppable sales team, you need to clear the (insert abrupt slang word here) out of your team's way so they can do their job. Not only will the team be more effective when you do, but their engagement and support for you, their leader, will also grow.

## BEING THE GATEKEEPER

When it comes to building a sales team that's unstoppable, as a leader, you are a gatekeeper. The irony of this statement is not lost on me, considering that most sales leaders spend their entire career attempting to find ways around gatekeepers.

As we discussed in earlier chapters, your sales team will only be as successful as the members who are part of it, so as the leader of the team, you need to be very selective as to who you let join the team and who is part of the team.

In addition to being selective about who joins and remains a part of the team, you'll need to manage new team member arrivals closely to ensure they quickly get up to speed and become part of the team. Your onboarding process must be robust enough to enable any new salesperson to hit the ground running, yet still be sufficiently collaborative to ensure they interact with all of the team members and those who they will be working with but aren't a part of the sales team.

In short, you need a solid onboarding plan that addresses these priorities, so work closely with your HR department to achieve this (note: never turn onboarding over to HR in its entirety, work with them instead to ensure the onboarding is effective for the new team member, and your team). Remember, this is your team member who you decided to hire, so their success is your responsibility. If you don't have an HR department, ask your other team members to assist in developing a sales playbook (i.e., resource that includes the sales process, best practices, and methods for success as a member of the team) for training and onboarding new sales team members. Having this resource as part of onboarding will make the process quick, painless, and effective.

### STORIES FROM THE SALES FLOOR

Many years ago, I worked with a medium-sized company. I was brought in to help turn the organization around from its slow financial decline. Not an easy feat by any shape of the imagination; however, among all the changes that we introduced, the most dramatic change we made was that of changes in the team members on their sales team.

Some examples of the changes we introduced included the following:

- Developed new sales processes incorporating input from the sales teams.
- Introduced stress tests to assess team members' performance in selling situations.
- Gained agreement on clear performance metrics to monitor team sales performance.
- Integrated a new CRM software to support the new sales processes.

Every one of these changes was made inclusive of the input, ideas, and feedback from team members. Nothing was introduced without agreement on the fact that the change was necessary, and that it would support (not hinder) the team's performance.

Despite the significance of these changes, the indirect impact of these changes was a complete rejuvenation of the sales team. Team members realized that long-term sustainability of the company (and their jobs) required we made significant changes in how we sold, and quickly.

We lost several team members through this process with some redeployed, some left, and others were asked to leave. Not an easy situation, but the team that remained was unstoppable.

Being the leader of an unstoppable sales team is not easy work; it can even seem unrewarding sometimes. But you must stay the course and remain focused on your goal of building a sales team that outperforms the competition.

Sound like a daunting task? It can be, but as the leader of an unstoppable sales team, you must have the courage and conviction to put the team and its continued improvement as your number one priority. In doing so, you'll face some tough decisions and actions that you'll need to take, for example:

- Help your team embrace your vivid vision of the future. Refer to it during discussions and team meetings.
- Identify your top performers and help them to grow further. Use their growth and skills to mentor and support those with lesser skills.
- Identify low performers and help them to expand their skills and performance. Continue to push lower performers to improve and don't ever back down. Complacency with low performance suggests acceptance of it.
- Take your time with decisions to redeploy or remove someone from the team. Make a solid assessment of their skills and fit with their role and within the team, and work to help them improve, but after 90 days, if you see no improvement, move them immediately.

For those who don't support your vision, your performance expectations, or the team (or the organization as a whole), your role, as tricky as it may seem, is to help the individual find a new position, department, or otherwise, that is a better fit for them. Your team and your subconscious will thank you for it.

Prioritize the redeployment of team members who aren't a fit to the same extent as you would finding team members that are a fit.

## DO YOU MAKE THE CUT? ASSESSING YOUR UNSTOPPABLE SALES LEADERSHIP CAPABILITIES

To this point, we've discussed the variety of responsibilities, strategies, and tactics a leader of an unstoppable sales team needs to embrace and make a part of their process. We've also discussed why each is important and what the outcome can be if you fail to follow through. So, when you consider all the priorities and tasks you'll need to complete to be successful as a leader of an unstoppable sales team, do I have what it takes?

Figure 9.2 provides an overview of the model, how to measure where you are today, and what is required to build and lead an unstoppable sales

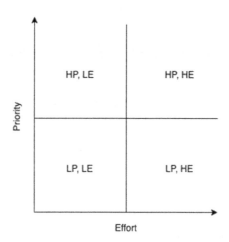

**FIGURE 9.2**

Measuring your unstoppable sales leader capabilities.

team successfully. First, score yourself and then use the score to identify where you need to focus your efforts in the list below.

## LOW PRIORITY, LOW EFFORT

In this quadrant, your leadership style and approach are farthest from that of an unstoppable leader. Begin by identifying the areas of most significant importance to the development of your team, create a plan, and execute step by step to begin the journey to improvement. It may take some time, but the good news is if you engage your team in the process, as I've suggested, they will recognize your efforts and support you along the way.

## LOW PRIORITY, HIGH EFFORT

In this quadrant, you are putting forth the effort required to build your team; however, your priorities and commitment to building an unstoppable team need to be clarified. First, you should revisit your priorities, determine the extent to which you need your team to be successful, and your role in helping them to become unstoppable. Then, develop a plan to shift your other possible competing priorities and place more emphasis on your team itself.

## HIGH PRIORITY, LOW EFFORT

If you fall into this quadrant, chances are you are treating every step of developing your team as a priority. As the old saying goes, if everything is a priority, then nothing is a priority. You need to step back, assess what's most important to introduce or change, and develop a new approach. Additionally, you can delegate tasks or steps that aren't a priority to ease some of the stress that can come with building a high-performing sales team. Lastly, create a triage system to assess new priorities or tasks that arise to ensure they don't make it to the top of your list and disrupt your progress.

## HIGH PRIORITY, HIGH EFFORT

In this quadrant, you are making the development of your team a priority, and you are placing sufficient effort into doing so. The key will be to remain in this quadrant. To do so, ensure you celebrate even the most minor successes or wins, involve your team in these celebrations, and continue practicing your methods to build the team. Just because you are where you need to be for success in building your team doesn't mean staying here is easy, so attack your progress just as seriously as if you were in any other quadrant.

## THE JOURNEY: BUILDING YOUR SKILLS AS AN UNSTOPPABLE SALES LEADER

Building an unstoppable sales team requires you to develop as a leader. In turn, building your team will require you to continuously focus on your self-improvement in conjunction with helping your team improve, individually and as a group. Use the following self-assessment questionnaire to determine where to focus your time and energy that will yield the most significant benefits for your team (and yourself). Answer these questions honestly, as anything less will provide you with a plan that isn't worth the paper it's written on.

## UNSTOPPABLE SALES LEADER SELF-ASSESSMENT

1. I place my team's success ahead of my success (Y/N).
2. I communicate daily with my sales team, engaging each member in the discussion (Y/N).

3. I am consistently improving my emotional intelligence and aware-ness (Y/N).
4. I periodically ask my team for honest feedback on how I can improve as a leader (Y/N).
5. I use any feedback I receive as an opportunity to improve (Y/N).
6. I have a plan that determines our progress as a stronger team (Y/N).
7. My goal is developed in collaboration with my team and is shared openly (Y/N).
8. I have a coach that helps me maintain perspective on my leadership development (Y/N).
9. My coach challenges me to think and behave differently (Y/N).
10. I celebrate even the small successes our team has along our journey (Y/N).

## Scoring

Give yourself one point for a Y (yes) and zero for an N (no). Then tally up your scores and use the following as a guide to what your next steps should be:

0–3: You are not demonstrating any of the behaviors we've discussed and have a tactical sales team, likely with poor morale and high turnover.

4–6: You are on the edge of becoming a leader of an unstoppable sales team, and with some effort and priority on the right areas, you can progress both yourself as a leader and your team's success.

7–10: You are well on your way to building an unstoppable sales team. Take time to reassess your priorities and align your time and energy with those that will have the most impact. Involve your team in this exercise to gain their input and support.

Now that we've laid out what it takes to build and lead an unstoppable sales team, do you have what it takes? Are you committed to this journey?

If you are, let's take a few minutes to identify how to use one of your most effective (and often misused) tools for leading a sales team, sales coaching.

**UNSTOPPABLE SALES TEAM ACTION STEPS:**

1. How strong is your emotional intelligence? What areas could you improve upon?
2. Which of the Unstoppable Sales Leader characteristics are you strongest in? What areas are you weakest in?
3. How are you supporting your sales team today as the gatekeeper? Is there more you can do?

For a printable copy of the Unstoppable Sales Team Leader Assessment, see www.unstoppablesales.team

Being a strong leader requires you have a method for getting the most from your sales team and coaching is your number one tool for doing so. In Chapter 10, let's discuss what being an effective coach for your unstoppable sales team requires.

# 10

Sales Coaching: A Framework for
Coaching an Unstoppable Sales Team

A coach is someone who can give correction without causing resentment.

**John Wooden**
*American Basketball Coach*

Leaders of unstoppable sales teams are first and foremost effective coaches, using their coaching skills as their primary means of building a coaching culture. As a sales leader then, being an effective coach is crucial to the team's success.

In this chapter, I will introduce you to my Unstoppable Sales[SM] Coaching model, a framework for coaching your sales team to achieve the highest levels of performance.

## TALKING IS NOT COACHING: HOW TO BUILD A FOUNDATION FOR EFFECTIVE COACHING

Having conversations with or speaking to your sales team does consititute coaching them. Coaching is a discipline that considers both the psychological and technical aspects of one's abilities in order to elevate their performance. So, pointing out weaknesses, sharing new selling methods, or asking questions about performance do not equate to sales coaching. Figure 10.1 outlines these differences.

DOI: 10.4324/9781003348610-13

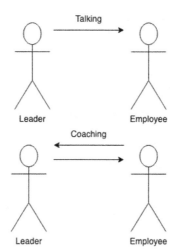

**FIGURE 10.1**
Talking versus coaching.

The objective of sales coaching (or any coaching, for that matter) is to evoke or elicit a change in behavior. If you achieve anything less than this, then the coaching is ineffective. This behavior change, then, becomes the measure of your ability to coach others successfully. Outside of a good framework for coaching, which we'll discuss in a moment, there are some fundamentals you'll need to consider if you want your coaching to be effective.

## SHAWN'S FOUNDATION FOR EFFECTIVE COACHING

Every person you coach is an individual, so your coaching approach will need to consider individual skills, behaviors, preferences, and mindsets. Your method for coaching should also consider the following:

1. Every individual has innate behaviors formed at a very young age, which generally do not change during their lifetime. Many studies, including the work of William Marston,[23] who published a book called *Emotions of Normal People* in 1928, and whose work informed the popular DiSC theory of behaviors.
2. Each person on your team has a dominant psychological function, namely sensation, intuition, feeling, and thinking, and one of

these functions is dominant most of the time. This theory is derived from the work of famed psychologist Carl Yung[24] and provides the basis for what is commonly known as MBTI or Myers–Briggs Type Indicator today.

3. Those experiences that have the most significant emotional impact on us are those we recall most prominently and which directly influence our needs, abilities, and desires. Essentially, we try to avoid situations or circumstances that we equate with pain or discomfort, and we seek out those situations or events we perceive will be comfortable.

Let me share an example. I used to own a Subaru WRX. It was a great car, had plenty of power, and was exciting to drive as it came with a six-speed standard transmission, requiring the driver to decide when and how to shift gears. I learned early on that first gear was almost useless if you were trying to get up to speed quickly. As quickly as you took off, you needed to shift to second gear almost immediately; otherwise, the car would actually hit the rev limiter and begin to slow down. So when I would get out of my WRX and jump into my wife's Toyota Tacoma, a V6 automatic 4 × 4, the driving experience was completely different. Not only did my left foot (my clutch foot) have nothing to do, but the speed at which I applied pressure to the gas pedal to accelerate was also entirely different.

Although I could drive both vehicles on the same road, they were similar in power and both moved me from point A to point B, reaching point B required completely different inputs on my part for each vehicle. In other words, each car operated differently and required me behave differently to achieve the same outcome (i.e., reaching point B).

Your objective for coaching each person on your sales team is to support them in selling and meeting their targets. Although each person may have similar experiences and education, and what motivates them may be identical (i.e., free time, stature, recognition, compensation, etc.), HOW you get them to perform requires a focus on the individuality of each person on the team.

Let's reconsider then my earlier point.

Having a discussion with someone on your sales team, telling them what they should be doing, or informing them what you want them to do is not coaching. This might sound obvious, however you'd be shocked at how many sales leaders, executives, and CEOs believe that telling someone what to do IS coaching. Coaching will only be effective if completed in a manner that considers the individual or individuals being coached. Keep this in mind as it pertains to your coaching, as it will guide you as a sales coach to adjust how you apply the pillars we're about to discuss.

I've been coaching individuals and sales teams for nearly 15 years; before that, I coached my staff across various industries and sectors, from unionized to non and young to mature. What I've learned during this time is that there are five pillars to coaching that provide a foundation for meaningful coaching that has an impact and evokes action.

## THE PILLARS FOR EFFECTIVE SALES COACHING

Although having a model for coaching makes sense, I'm focusing first on the five fundamental pillars upon which you'll want to build your sales coaching. My reasoning is every model you encounter (including the one I layout below) will need some adjustments or changes to accommodate your unique circumstances. This is NOT what you'll be told by those trying to sell or certify you in their coaching model, but as my mentor, Alan Weiss[25] says, *"who certifies the certifiers?"*

## SHAWN'S PILLARS FOR EFFECTIVE COACHING

Figure 10.2 provides an overview of these pillars as part of my Unstoppable Sales[SM] coaching model. However, applying these pillars requires that you consider each pillar as part of your preparation for the coaching conversation as follows:

1. **Awareness:** You should begin all coaching conversations with a question that confirms if the coachee is aware of whether there is a change or improvement necessary.
2. **Benefit:** There must be a benefit to making a personal change in our behavior. Examples might include better or faster results that serve us, higher closing ratios, more significant margins, fewer objections, ease of building relationships, more enjoyable interactions with

**Pillars of Effective Sales Coaching**

| Awareness | Benefit | Belief | Ability | Results |
|---|---|---|---|---|
| | | | | |

**FIGURE 10.2**
Pillars of effective sales coaching.

co-workers, etc. If I can see a benefit to your feedback, I'm more apt to change my behavior.

3. **Belief:** There must be a belief that I have the skills and tools to introduce a change. If you suggest that I change my behavior, yet I don't believe the change is possible and am closed-minded to the change, then I'm unlikely to make the change. Good coaching includes creating the belief that change is possible by sharing how others have introduced and been successful with the exact change.

4. **Ability:** There must be a perception that I can change my behavior. I must have access to and be able to apply various resources, knowledge, tools, and information that support my ability to achieve the desired behavior. One can improve their ability through observation and application of new skills, including demonstrations, trials, tests, or pilots.

5. **Results:** If my behavior change is to sustain, I must realize results. Results that satisfy the earlier pillars convince me that a change in my behavior is necessary to achieve the desired outcomes. Additionally, results, whether expected or different than expected, demonstrate the impact of a change in our behavior on products, reinforcing the need to continue making minor adjustments in our behavior rather than incremental change.

When you use these pillars as part of every coaching conversation, you ensure that your coaching is effective, pursuing results individualized for each person on your team. As you become comfortable with these pillars, they'll become a natural means for approaching your sales coaching. In the meantime, consider each pillar in the order described for your upcoming coaching conversations. Doing so will support you in transitioning your existing coaching to a more effective one.

## UNSTOPPABLE SALES COACHING MODEL

Now that we've identified the pillars of effective sales coaching, let's talk about a model for you to use that encourages behavioral change and empowers your sales team to apply new skills and be excited about seeking improvement in their performance.

Let me first tell you how this model came to be. Beginning in my early teens at my first job at A&P, then concluding at my last official "job" before launching my speaking and consulting business in 2009, I've had just over 20 different bosses. That's approximately one new boss each year, and I can assure you that each of them had a different approach to coaching, or at least what they thought was coaching. These different employer–employee relationships allow me to identify what worked well for me, and others, in a wide array of industries.

As a result, a common framework for coaching emerged, which I began to apply at the early age of 23 when I started leading my first official team. Since this time, I've continued improving the model as I transitioned from applying it with my team to educating others on its application through consulting and coaching work, making improvements based on the experiences of those who have applied it.

The result is what I refer to as the Unstoppable Sales$^{SM}$ Coaching model, a proven method for sales leaders to support their teams in recognizing how they can tap into their unique strengths and abilities to become unstoppable. Let me make it abundantly clear here: anyone who can already sell can reach new performance levels with this model. The model builds self-confidence by applying new skills that can, in turn, remove self-limiting beliefs and propel performance to new levels.

There are a variety of coaching models out there, so before I share the one I've found to be most effective, let's clarify how it's different from others you might have come across.

First, much of the coaching that sales leaders provide their teams focus on tactical aspects of the sales process. The goal is to keep behavior the same but to provide support and feedback that the sales professional can apply, improving their sales results. This type of coaching can be effective; however, it rarely sustains new skills over the long term. Examples of this type of coaching include the following:

**Prospect coaching:** This coaching focuses on the activity of prospecting. Coaching focuses on identifying methods and steps to identify, find, and connect with prospects to generate more opportunities to generate new business.

**Deal coaching:** This coaching focuses on supporting a sales professional in successfully closing a deal. Examples may include helping to overcome objections and delays and providing insights and skills to close the deal. An example is a sales professional asking their manager for assistance to close a deal.

**Objection coaching:** This coaching applies when the sales professional struggles to overcome specific objections such as price. The sales leader shares insights and tools to overcome these objections and keep the deal moving forward.

**Pipeline coaching:** This coaching is often very tactical and includes a review of the sales professional's pipeline of deals, sharing insights, suggestions, and strategies to keep deals moving to close.

Most other coaching models out there are designed to be broadly applicable. Common examples include the GROW (Goal, Reality, Options and Will) coaching model by Sir John Whitmore,[26] or the OSKAR (Outcome, Scale, Know-how, Affirm + Action, and Review) model by Paul Jackson and Mark McKergow, outlined in their book Solutions Focus.[27] I've found that although these models can be somewhat effective, they fail to take into account the unique and individual circumstances of each organization and the objectives of the leader who is applying them (Figure 10.3).

**Unstoppable Sales Team Coaching Model**

**FIGURE 10.3**
Unstoppable sales coaching model.

---

## SHAWN'S UNSTOPPABLE SALES COACHING MODEL

### Stage #1: Desired Outcome

In this first stage, we paint a picture of success. What is the desired outcome? How will we know when we have achieved it?

### Stage #2: Objectives

With outcomes clarified, we next discuss objectives. What are the critical goals that we must achieve to meet the outcomes?

### Stage #3: Individual Needs

With outcomes identified, the next step is the discussion of needs. What does the coachee believe they need to be successful? Examples might include skills, support, tools, or other resources.

### Stage #4: Perceived Barriers

Once needs have been discussed, it's essential to tackle perceived barriers. At this stage, you don't accept the obstacles; instead, you attempt to uncover the challenges for the coachee, whether real or perceived. Doing so will allow you to either assist in overcoming them through skills, practice, or additional coaching. Alternatively, if the perceived barriers are unlikely, you'll need to share information and examples that dispel these concerns.

### Stage #5: Milestones

This last step is the most important. For each objective you identify, significant milestones will be necessary to ensure successful progress. These milestones should be discussed and monitored as part of progress.

With the steps identified, let's look at how the model works using common examples that you'll likely face with your sales team.

#### Example #1: Improve Conversion Ratio

In this scenario, your sales team member needs to convert deals at the rate you expect (and has been proven achievable). Here are the steps you would take using the Unstoppable Sales Coaching model.

*Desired Outcome*

Deals convert at X% (an increase over the current rate).

*Objectives*

Objectives may include increasing the number of conversion discussions, better preparation for each conversion discussion, and improved handling of common objections.

*Individual Needs*

Following the discussion on desired outcomes and objectives, the next step is to have an open dialogue to determine what the person being coached needs to achieve the objectives. The key here is the dialogue being "open," which means you'll share your view on what will be required and solicit what the salesperson believes they need. In this example, everyday needs shared by the manager (you) might include training on handling objections, more time scheduled for conversion meetings, etc. The coachee might share a desire to sit in on a peer's conversion meetings to observe their approach and eliminate some administrative tasks that reduce the time available to hold conversion meetings.

*Perceived Barriers*

Similar to the discussion of individual needs, you'll want to explore any perceived barriers that the coachee has. In our example above, some perceived barriers might include insufficient experience in handling conversion discussions, a lack of skills to deal with some of the objections faced, and poor quality of prospects resulting in a lower percentage of deals converted.

*Milestones*

Typical milestones in this example might include blocking additional time for their conversion calls, a list of common objections and responses to review and practice, and a weekly review meeting to review conversion progress and discuss any obstacles.

### Example #2: Increase Prospecting Activity

Let's say you need someone on your sales team to increase their prospecting activity. Let's use the model to frame this as a coaching conversation.

### Desired Outcomes

The desired outcome would be to have X percent of time dedicated to prospecting each week, month, and year.

### Objectives

The objectives to achieve the outcome include blocking out a specific amount of time each week for prospecting activities, identifying and consistently applying the most effective prospecting activities, and increasing the number of prospects pursued each week.

### Individual Needs

Through the discussion of the needs, you'll want to understand what the coachee believes will be necessary for them to achieve these outcomes. For example, what is their starting point? What tools or resources will be essential to achieve these outcomes? Examples of what would likely arise in this discussion include better-qualified leads, more time available in their day to focus on prospecting, better software to support prospecting, etc.

### Perceived Barriers

Following the discussion of the individual needs, what are the barriers that the individual perceives may hold them back or limit that success? Examples of barriers might include lack of time available, insufficient software or other tools, poor quality of information from marketing, etc.

### Milestones

Finally, what milestones will confirm the pursuit of the objectives and consistent progress? Examples might include creating and sharing a new touch point strategy, time blocked each week for prospecting activities, weekly reporting on prospects contacted, and prospects moved to the proposal or quote stage.

As you can tell from these steps, there is nothing earth-shattering about using the Unstoppable Sales[SM] Coaching model. What the model does provide, however, is a framework for successful coaching outcomes. Too often as sales leaders, we often need to dive deeper into understanding the coachee's perspectives, beliefs, or concerns. As a result, our coaching could be more practical. When we use the framework outlined above, we have more involvement by the coachee and, as a result, a better opportunity for successful coaching outcomes, which, last I checked, is the measure of successful coaching.

## COMBINING SALES COACHING WITH FEEDBACK FOR GREATER IMPACT

Even if you have a solid coaching model, your coaching will still be effective. So, in this last section, let's discuss some areas that can be either complimentary or detrimental to your coaching efforts and how to ensure there is more of the former than the latter.

Too often, I come across sales leaders consistently providing feedback to their sales team, thinking that it's coaching, and frustrated that there is no impact. Although this may seem basic, let me clarify the differences.

Coaching is proactive, painting a picture of a desired future state. Alternatively, feedback is reactive and provides information after the fact.

Both improve future performance, but as you'll notice from the points above, feedback is reflective and after the fact, meaning that there is a chance the discussion will only be remembered after the next opportunity to apply its lessons emerges. Coaching, on the other hand, happens before a meeting, situation, or circumstance, focusing on being timely and preparing the sales professional for what's to come.

In other words, as a sales leader, although you use feedback and coaching, the former is better used as a positive reinforcement tool. In contrast, the latter, coaching, is better for informing and supporting high performance. For this reason, I don't spend more time discussing feedback in this book. However, if you want to build an unstoppable sales team, you must become a highly effective coach for your sales team, using feedback as a positive reinforcement tool.

## YOU AS A COACH: ASSESSING GAPS IN YOUR OWN COACHING

It's also important to mention in this chapter that although you might use the framework above to coach your sales team, you need to be aware of your personal beliefs, perspectives, and limitations. In other words, not everyone is born an effective coach, and identifying the gaps and areas for improvement in your coaching is critical to the impact it will have on others.

There are four areas to consider as it pertains to becoming an effective coach, they are:

1. Your motivation
2. Your preferred communication
3. Your mindset

## Motivation

If you are motivated to coach your sales team to support your objectives, such as a higher commission or increased recognition, your ability to coach will always be clouded by your judgment. I've seen too many coaches attempt to coach others and become frustrated when their coaching is ineffective, mainly because of the personal impact the poor performance of others has.

Those who are successful in coaching a sales team are because of their desire to see others succeed, plain and simple.

## Communication

If you prefer to communicate in methods that are effective for you rather than the coachee, your coaching will be ineffective. I am a visual communicator, so I do well when pictures or drawings are shared; however, I expect those I coach to be different.

Successful coaches ask their coaches how they prefer to communicate, identify individual preferences, then use those to drive home discussions and ensure receptivity on the part of the coachee.

## Mindset

If your view is that sales professionals are born, not built, or that learning new skills is impossible (recall our earlier discussions on fixed versus growth mindset), then it's your coaching will be ineffective.

Successful coaches possess a mindset that others can be successful in sales if given the right tools, knowledge, support, and time, and they recognize that these are unique to every person they coach.

As a coach, you need to constantly improve your abilities to coach others, focusing specifically on your motivation, communication, and mindset. In other words, it's not enough to apply the model above and expect results. For example, leaders of unstoppable sales teams see themselves as being coachable and seek to coach themselves to continue overcoming their weaknesses and vulnerabilities.

#### UNSTOPPABLE SALES TEAM ACTION STEPS:

1. Which of the pillars are a strength for you currently?
2. Are there areas you should improve as a coach? What steps can you take to do so?
3. How closely does the Unstoppable Sales Coaching model mimic your current coaching methods? What improvements or changes should you make?
4. How are you balancing your use of feedback versus coaching with your sales team?

If you'd like a printable version of the Unstoppable Sales Coaching model, see www.unstoppablesales.team

# 11

## Setting Sales Performance Metrics That Matter

Do what you love, and do it well—that's much more meaningful than any metric.

**Kevin Systrom**
*American Computer Programmer*

Selling is an activity-based role, meaning the more activity a sales professional engages in, the greater the likelihood they'll generate new sales. For this reason, many sales executives and leaders use metrics that measure activities rather than the value and results of the measures themselves. They tend to set metrics in a way that doesn't recognize the individuality of people on their teams, often resulting in a lack of buy-in by their team to pursue (and achieve) the metrics.

In this chapter, we'll discuss the sales metrics to avoid using and, most importantly, identify the factors to consider when setting metrics to make sure they motivate your sales team.

## WHAT GETS MEASURED DOESN'T ALWAYS GET IMPROVED

Early in my career, while leading a small sales team, I wanted to create more consistent results among our sales team. After several months on the job, it became apparent there were some considerable gaps in how each

DOI: 10.4324/9781003348610-14

team member approached sales, so setting some sales performance metrics would level the playing field.

I chose the standard measures you'll find being used with most sales teams today, such as the number of prospects generated, the number of deals created, the number of sales closed, the number of referrals obtained, etc. To my surprise, despite developing, introducing, and monitoring these metrics, my sales team continued to approach selling differently. Some were great at generating and closing new leads; however, their desire and ability to support existing customer (with whom new sales opportunities existed) were virtually nonexistent, resulting in no referrals. Others seemed to spend excessive time socializing with their prospects and customers. A few seemed almost to shy away from selling, preferring to spend most of their time hiding behind email. Lastly, a few overly focused on research, spending much of their time prepping for meetings and attempting to write the perfect proposal, resulting in very few sales.

Although the sales metrics I chose were quite common and measured vital areas of our sales process, they failed to consider the individuality of members of the sales team. Each metric had a different meaning to everyone on the team, depending on their experience, knowledge, behavior, and preferences. As a result, measures alone did nothing to create the behaviors and actions I sought from the group and, in some cases, hindered performance. The lesson learned was that I must customize sales metrics for the team and each member if I expected them to impact individual performance.

## SHAWN'S RULES FOR SALES METRICS

1. Measures don't change behaviors—they identify them.
2. There must be a mix of both common team measures and individualized measures.
3. Each team professional must be involved in selecting their performance measures.
4. Each team member should assess their performance as the sales leader observes.
5. Avoid using accusatory statements when asking questions about performance.

6. Tie suggestions for improvement to real-world examples and observations.
7. Everyone (including the sales leader) is responsible for the team's performance.
8. Failure to meet performance measures is rarely the result of a singular issue.
9. Discussions about improving individual performance should be behind closed doors.
10. The sales leader should also have and report on their own performance measures.

Applying these rules will ensure that team members accept and adopt your performance measures. The goal is to have any performance measures perceived to identify gaps and opportunities rather than a hammer to hit people over the head when they don't perform.

## CHOOSING SALES METRICS THAT MATTER

When you transition from grade school through college, you likely recall that how each of your teachers or professors grade you, what they grade you on, and how they report and share this information, changes. Essentially, as you evolve and grow as an individual, expectations of your performance increase in parallel; we need to use this same philosophy with the performance measures for our sales team.

Our sales metrics must also evolve with the development of our team. As sales leaders, the performance and behaviors we expect of our team should change and evolve as our customers, the business, the environment, and the individuals on our team evolve.

Reasons for this evolution may include:

- Development of the sales professional.
- New levels of performance achieved by the sales team.
- Changes in the business climate or market.
- Growth of the business, its products, and services.
- Shifts in markets or customers served.

To select the right sales metrics for both the team and the individuals on the team, we must consider all these factors and ask ourselves what the priorities in our sales strategy are and what behaviors we need to encourage, support, and monitor to achieve this strategy. There are obviously a wide variety of standard sales measures you can choose from, although each will have to be personalized and sensitized to your team, the people it impacts, and your strategic sales objectives.

The most common sales measures to consider include:

- Sales targets (daily, weekly, monthly, annually).
- New sales generated/closed.
- Calls/emails/outreach per time period.
- New sales opportunities created.
- Presentation/demo meetings booked.
- Lead conversion rate.
- Sales generated by contact method.
- Average time to close.
- Average deal size/sale value.
- Customer acquisition cost (CAC).
- Customer lifetime value (LTV).
- Monthly reoccurring revenue (MRR).
- Pipeline value/number of deals in the pipeline.
- Sales by territory or region.
- Average profit margin.
- Average revenue generated.
- Win rate or close ratio.
- Deal conversion rate.
- Average profit margin.
- Loss rate.
- Average deal size.
- Sales cycle length.
- Customer retention rate.
- Customer resell/upsell rate.

To be clear, you don't need all these measures, and I'm sure there are several I've missed here; however, these are the most common and relevant measures to consider. You can also apply these measures to an individual and a team.

The next step in selecting which measures support the desired behaviors and performance, considering the current state of business, and the strategic goals and objectives you've set for the sales team, is to consider the following questions, the responses to which will inform your selection of measures.

1. What is the top priority for our company today (i.e., sales growth, customer retention, profit margin, etc.)? Select one.
2. What are the behaviors and actions that sales must deliver to achieve our main priority (i.e., open new markets, pursue fortune 500 companies, reduce time to close, etc.)?
3. What measures will monitor and support your team in consistently pursuing these behaviors (i.e., finding new prospects weekly, increasing deal size, maintaining a target profit margin, etc.)?

With the answers prepared, you can now determine which measures make sense individually versus those that apply on a team basis. You may want to monitor and report on some measures at both levels, such as Monthly Sales Revenue Generated or New Leads Generated.

## DYNAMIC VERSUS STATIC MEASURES

Something that many sales leaders don't consider when setting their sales team's measures is the degree to which the measures are dynamic. As your sales strategy, goals, business climate, team dynamic, or even the sales team's skills evolve, you'll want to review and update your measures to identify when they should change. Most sales leaders perceive measures as static (i.e., something that is set once and will sustain regardless of changes in the market, improved skills of the sales team, etc.). As a result, the lack of adjustment to their measures over time only serves to lessen the measures' impact and increase the team's complacency and frustration.

Use measures to refresh and rejuvenate your team maintaining their attention on what matters most and reflecting changes both inside and outside of their control.

## LEADING VERSUS LAGGING MEASURES

Performance measures you set should be a combination of lagging and leading indicators. If all your measures report on what has already happened (Monthly Revenue Generated, Monthly Deals Converted, etc.), it does nothing but tell you what has already happened. It's like driving to a destination while looking out your rear-view mirror. You know where you've been but not where you're going.

Having lagging measures tells us how we did, but we also need leading indicators to tell us if we are on the right path. Some examples, using our list above, of leading indicators, include:

- New Sales Generated (i.e., are sales trending as we intend?).
- Discovery Meetings Booked (i.e., what sales opportunities are before us?).
- New Leads Identified (i.e., are we pursuing the right leads?).
- Sales Generated by Contact Method (i.e., which contact methods are increasingly effective?).

There are others you can incorporate, so when selecting or updating your measures, ask yourself, are these lagging indicators of how we've performed or leading indicators of where we are going?

With leading and lagging measures now selected, let's discuss how to use these measures to improve individual performance.

## METRICS THAT MOTIVATE INDIVIDUAL PERFORMANCE

So far, we've discussed the importance of individual and team performance measures and the nuances of each. For a moment, let's dive deeper into using measures to motivate individual performance.

You'll recall our discussion on Maslow's Hierarchy of Needs[28] and the individual nature of how we define and prioritize our needs. We also briefly touched on the work of William Marston[29] and his theories on human behavior.

Although you'll need to choose measures that provide you with the information you need from your team, you will also need to design and introduce measures that motivate the individuals on your team to perform, influencing them to adopt new methods and strategies. If you are like most of the sales leaders I coach, your default position will be to have common measures that you use for 80% of your sales team, and then some special measures for the 20% of your sales team that don't perform at the level you expect. But, unfortunately, there's a problem with this approach.

If you want to retain your sales team, particularly high performers, you'll need measures that challenge them to grow. Ignoring someone who exceeds their sales quota each month because they are doing well is not the right approach. My findings have been that high-performing sales professionals need more challenge and opportunity than those who perform poorly. This might seem counterintuitive, but assuming you were once a high-performing sales professional, didn't you find that boredom crept in once you figured out the best method to sell whatever it was you were selling?

At this point, you're probably considering jumping to Chapter 12 because this seems like a lot of work. However, it doesn't have to be when you realize that your sales team consists of three main categories of performers. Some perform below expectations; some will consistently meet your expectations, and there will be some who repeatedly exceed your expectations. Use Figure 11.1 to identify these for each of your team members.

Using this method to identify individual performance measures is a simple and effective means of ensuring you pick measures that motivate higher performance levels regardless of how well your team member is doing. Additionally, you must invest your time equally across your sales team to move each person to higher performance levels.

What typically happens is that we spend 80% of our time with 20% of the team members who need to achieve our expectations. This model encourages us to be more strategic about investing our time with our sales team. So, although some team members may need less coaching relative to methods to achieve their performance measures, we can't assume that once we introduce some individual measures, they will automatically be adopted and inspire higher performance levels.

| Assessing Team Performance Levels |
|---|
| **Below Expectations** |
| **Meet Expectations** |
| **Exceed Expectations** |

**FIGURE 11.1**
Assessing sales team performance.

## TEAM PERFORMANCE MEASURES THAT MATTER (AND MOTIVATE!)

When I sold cars early in my career, there was a large chart on the back of the sales manager's door. At the top of the chart, from left to right, were ten individual car images, with another five images in a different color, totaling 15 cars. Our names were alphabetically along the left side, from top to bottom. For each new car we sold, the sales manager (who always had the final say on every deal) would put a checkmark under a car next to our name. Then, at the end of the month, he would total up the number of vehicles we sold and mention this at our sales meeting.

He never formally introduced the chart to us, but invariably it only took a couple of closed-door meetings, most often to discuss a pending deal, for each sales team member to notice the chart. Curious one day, I asked him why the change of color in the last 5 of 15 cars, to which he responded by telling me that there was a bonus for every car we sold that extended beyond ten vehicles. I then asked him if someone had sold 15 cars in a month, to which he replied that it was rare but possible.

This conversation was the closest we ever got to discussing my performance and how I might improve it, possibly even to reach the elusive 15 cars per month (although I was called into his office on a few occasions when I lost a sale). Sure, there was the monthly sales meeting in which we learned about new car features and future models, during which we reviewed the number of cars sold for the previous month, but that was it. I received nothing in the form of individual performance measures and no direct coaching about how I might improve my performance.

A couple of people in our dealership loved the chart, and just looking at those checkmarks added up next to their name did motivate them to sell more. But for the majority, the chart and the lack of individual discussions and coaching to help us reach the elusive 15 cars were more de-motivating than motivating.

I eventually left the dealership, moving to selling other products and leaving the automotive industry behind. Although my experience was decades ago, it went the way of many automotive sales professionals today. A study by the Cox group[30] recently confirmed turnover among automotive sales professionals to be at 46%, which is not surprising considering my experience.

You need to take several steps if you want the performance measures you set to generate enthusiasm with your team and support them in moving to higher levels of performance. I call these the rules for creating performance measures that matter.

## SHAWN'S RULES FOR PERFORMANCE MEASURES THAT MATTER

1. Involve each member of your team in the selection of measures designed to improve their performance.
2. Hold frequent coaching conversations to review progress and introduce new ideas and methods to improve performance.
3. Reinforce the individual value of performance measures to everyone supporting them with your observations and examples.

4. Consistently refer to the measures in one-on-one conversations, group discussions, and meetings.
5. Change measures when they no longer seem relevant at the individual level or aren't achieving the intended performance levels.
6. Review and update team measures annually, aligning them to your sales strategy.
7. Consider any feedback or ideas your employees have on improving or changing measures.
8. Keep team measures visible to everyone, updating progress weekly at a minimum (daily, if possible).
9. Share measures outside your department, educating other departments on the goals and targets for sales.
10. Involve other departments or functions in your sales meeting when they directly or indirectly impact measures (i.e., bring in marketing to discuss the quality of leads).

When you set the right measures on an individual and team basis, you develop a pathway to higher performance levels. So now, let's take these measures and dive into some additional proven methods to accelerate your sales team's performance.

### UNSTOPPABLE SALES TEAM ACTION STEPS:

1. What are the common measures you are using with your sales team today?
2. What changes will you make to these measures considering what we've discussed?
3. How will you ensure you maintain dynamic measures that are forward focused?
4. What steps will you take to introduce these measures in a way that will motivate your team, and the individuals on it?

For a list of commonly applied individual and team performance measures, see www.unstoppablesales.team

# 12

## Technology to Accelerate Your Sales Team's Performance

The first rule of any technology used in a business is that automation applied to an efficient operation will magnify the efficiency. The second is that automation applied to an inefficient operation will magnify the inefficiency.

**Bill Gates**
*American Business Magnate*

As I begin writing this chapter, it strikes me that some of you may have skipped previous chapters and started at Chapter 12. There's a chance that your sales team is performing well, but you want to understand what technology you can introduce to help them sell more, sell faster, and be more effective as a team.

If that's your goal, then fortunately you've come to the right place, and we'll start by discussing some of the most crucial technology you'll want to consider if your team is already performing at near unstoppable levels (my bias is, if you don't pursue any improvements other than what you take from this chapter, then your team won't truly reach the unstoppable levels we've been discussing). I wrote this book to be your step-by-step playbook for building a high-performing sales team that is unstoppable, so if you jumped to this chapter, make sure you go back and invest some time catching up on the previous chapters.

DOI: 10.4324/9781003348610-15

## THE THREE PHASES OF SALES TEAM MATURITY

Before we dive into how to accelerate your sales team's performance, we first need to take stock of where your team is today. As your team progresses, the technology you should focus on to accelerate your sales team's performance will evolve and change.

For example, the methods and approaches to help a newly formed sales team accelerate their performance are very different than those of a more mature sales team that has worked together for many years. Additionally, as your team transitions from newly formed to mature, the methods you invoke to accelerate performance further will need to evolve with your team.

When our dog Charlie was young, he was a bundle of energy, and training was difficult. He wouldn't stay in one place long enough to attempt to train him on new skills; however, later in life, Charlie is a much calmer dog, has significantly more patience, and is more likely to listen to our instructions. Although Charlie is more attentive today, training him on new skills is still challenging, not because he is a bundle of energy but because he has formed habits that must be re-programmed. For the record however, training him with new skills is still possible (remember what I said earlier, you *can* teach an old dog new tricks); it just requires some patience.

The processes, measures, coaching, and technology for building an unstoppable sales team can differ depending on the maturity of your sales team. For example, suppose you are in a start-up or newer company with an immature sales process. In this case, your focus will be on enabling your team to sell while learning and applying new sales processes and forming peer and mentor relationships. The steps and methods you'll use to lead a fully developed and mature sales team, where proven sales processes and technology already exist, are quite different.

The objective then is to identify what changes or improvements will further elevate your team's performance. Figure 12.1 depicts the three different stages.

Let's look at each stage and how you as a leader can accelerate the team's performance through each stage, transitioning the team to new levels of performance. First you will need to determine which stage aligns with where your sales team are today.

**FIGURE 12.1**
Three stages of sales team maturity.

1. **Newly formed sales team:** This team consists of at least 50% new sales team members.
   The focus areas for accelerating the performance of your team include the following:

| Sales process | Measures/metrics | Coaching | Technology | Culture |
|---|---|---|---|---|
| Primary | Secondary | Secondary | Tertiary | Primary |

   **Summary:** The key focus areas for a newly minted sales team are to formulate and educate around a consistent and effective sales process while building a solid team culture. Having measures for performance and using coaching to achieve those metrics is secondary as the team and the sales process begin to develop.

2. **Growing sales team:** This team has existed and worked together for over 2 years and has less than 80% new members during the last 6 months. The company has been in operation for more than 5 years. The focus areas for accelerating the performance of your sales team include the following:

| Sales process | Measures/metrics | Coaching | Technology | Culture |
|---|---|---|---|---|
| Tertiary | Secondary | Primary | Secondary | Primary |

**Summary:** With a growing sales team, the predominance of your sales team have been in the sales department for several years, and the sales processes are mature and effective. In this instance, the focus should be on coaching to improve performance, supported by suitable measures and more advanced technology that supports (not hinders) sales team performance. The focus remains on building a strong team culture to retain top performers.

3. **Mature sales team:** This team has worked together for more than 5 years and has less than 70% new members during the last 6 months. The company has been in operation for more than 10 years.

The focus areas for accelerating the performance of your team include the following:

| Sales process | Measures/metrics | Coaching | Technology | Culture |
|---|---|---|---|---|
| Tertiary | Tertiary | Primary | Primary | Primary |

**Summary:** For the mature sales team, the processes and measures used have been proven effective over an extended period of time. Improvements in the efficiency or effectiveness of the sales processes in this instance are mostly likely to result from introducing technology. Coaching as a primary means of performance improvement and a continued focus on building a solid team culture (to retain top performers) remains a key focus.

## TECHNOLOGY TO SUPPORT BUILDING YOUR UNSTOPPABLE SALES TEAM

There are hundreds, if not thousands, of software options and technology that you can introduce to improve the performance of your sales team. Having worked with a wide variety of sales teams globally, what I've learned to be true is that not all technology is good technology, and the decision as to whether a new piece of technology will aid or hinder sales team performance should always be that of the sales team. Put differently, departments outside sales, such as Finance, Operations, Customer Service, IT, or others, should not have the final decision on whether the sales team adopts new technology; that decision must ultimately lie with the team itself, facilitated by yourself as the leader. I explain this and other key insights in my laws for sales team technology adoption.

## SHAWN'S LAWS OF TECHNOLOGY ADOPTION FOR SALES TEAMS

1. Technology must complement (not hinder) existing sales team processes.
2. Any technology adopted must act as an aid that increases sales productivity or performance.
3. More technology is not always a good thing.
4. Technology that aids in reporting but reduces efficiency is useless.
5. The sales team is the final decision maker on whether technology is adopted.
6. Any technology used must integrate seamlessly with other technology in use.
7. Review technology annually to ensure continued effectiveness and usefulness.

### STORIES FROM THE SALES FLOOR

I did some work with an insurance company who had a large team of agents spread across the country. The owner had purchased a very reputable (and expensive) software that was designed to handle all the operational transactions for insurance companies.

The software included a CRM (Customer Relationship Management) module which was clearly an add-on and acted as nothing more than an excel spreadsheet. Names and contact information could be added, but that is about it. The agents, many of whom had been exposed to other common (and much more effective) CRM software had been begging the President to purchase a separate CRM, and had even agreed on one that they wanted, which it turns out would easily integrate with the software that was already being used.

The President, having made a significant investment in the software, was completely against any additional software.

After working with the sales team, I suggested to the President that testing the new CRM system, which had a low monthly cost per user, would be a wise decision. He was skeptical at first, until I confirmed it would complement his existing operational software, didn't require any customization to be effective, would provide significantly more information for reporting on sales and selling activities, and was a cheap investment in retaining his team of agents.

He agreed to the test and within a week made the decision (and investment) to purchase the new software. To this day his team is still using that CRM software and loving it. Their productivity has improved on account of the additional features for helping them track and complete specific tasks, and the information collected has helped to pinpoint areas for improvement within their sales process.

When I met with the President recently and asked how the team was doing, he responded that the new CRM software was providing him with additional information on the sales team's performance he wasn't able to previously access and that it was the best decision he could have made.

Considering there are hundreds of different technology and software solutions that you can introduce to aid in the productivity and performance of your sales team, I've consolidated these into a list for you to reference as you deem necessary. A quick disclaimer or warning if you will: Any names of software that I share are for example purposes only. I've seen many examples of software and technology used for similar purpose and to be highly effective, so this isn't intended to sway your decision in any way, nor am I brand loyal or sponsored by any of these companies. As with any software, invest and use at your own risk. Your unique situation may result in some software not working well, so always do your own testing and research (with your sales team!) before you ever make any investment in technology.

## TECHNOLOGY TO BOOST YOUR SALES TEAM'S PERFORMANCE

Some of you are excited about this section but before we dive in, let me state what may seem obvious, and that is that technology is a tool. I discuss other examples of technology to aid in improving your sales processes in my book *The Unstoppable Sales Machine*, so for our purposes here, let's focus on technology that aids in making your sales team unstoppable rather than technology that supports your sales process. I've witnessed many sales teams who are less than pleased after their leadership thrust on them some miracle software that was intended to improve their performance, but in fact altered their methods of working, ultimately reducing their productivity while increasing their frustration.

There are four main areas in which technology that aids your team to perform at unstoppable levels can be categorized, namely:

**Technology to aid with prospecting:** Some examples of software that will support prospecting include the following:
1. Software to assist in finding new leads (i.e., ZoomInfo[31]).
2. Video software to assist in prospect outreach (i.e., BombBomb[32]).
3. Software to support automated email follow-up (i.e., Active Campaign[33]).
4. Software to capture online leads for sales (i.e., Tidio[34]).
5. Software to aid in social media prospecting (i.e., CoPilot AI[35]).

**Technology for managing information:** Examples of technology that can aid in collecting and managing customer and prospect information include the following:
1. CRM (Customer Resource Management) software (i.e., Salesforce[36])
2. Apps for collecting prospect information while on the go (i.e., Spotio[37])
3. Document-sharing platforms (i.e., Dropbox[38])
4. Software to support electronic contracts and signatures (i.e., PandaDoc[39])

**Technology for developing and delivering presentations:** Software for use with presentations both in-person and virtually includes the following:
1. Digital meeting platforms (i.e., Zoom[40])
2. Slide deck software (i.e., Keynote[41])
3. Software for conducting virtual surveys (i.e., SurveyMonkey[42])

**Technology for improving sales team productivity:** Examples of software that are designed to improve your sales team's productivity include:
1. Apps to support group discussions and sharing (i.e., WhatsApp[43]).
2. Software to aid with information and document sharing (i.e., Circle[44]).

3. Software to assist with sales strategy and planning (i.e., Trello[45]).
4. Gamification software to support achieving goals (i.e., Hoopla[46]).
5. Software for performance measurement and tracking (i.e., Brainshark[47]).
6. Software to aid in prospect and customer outreach (i.e., Outreach[48]).

Whatever your need, guaranteed there is software out there that can help. The real question you must consider is whether the software aids or hinders your sales team's performance, and they are the only ones that can tell you if this is the case. One thing you will notice, however, is that there are people on your sales team who are excited about the idea of introducing new software and others who aren't. To overcome these two competing forces, use the following assessment to identify and introduce software that will support your team.

**Shawn's Software Selection Criteria:**

1. Define the current objective (i.e., are you trying to increase the number and quality of prospects and improve the responsiveness of your sales team with prospects?).
2. Identify software options that:
   • Have a strong reputation in your industry or sector.
   • Support or enhance your existing sales processes.
   • Have users with whom you can speak to verify functionality and benefits.
   • Integrate well with your other critical software and technology.
3. Identify a pilot or test of the software with a small group of your sales team that are typically early adopters of the software.
4. Share the results of the pilot (as it progresses) with your sales team (if it goes well, this will help with broad adoption).
5. Only move forward with technology your team is satisfied with and meets the criteria.

I could write a book on sales technology (and maybe I will!); however, given that our focus is on supporting you in building an unstoppable sales team, let's settle on the fact that any technology introduced should aid in your mission to improve your sales team's performance is a far more strategic approach to introducing technology.

## INTRODUCING NEW TECHNOLOGY TO SUPPORT YOUR SALES TEAM'S PERFORMANCE

Aside from using the selection criteria above to determine what software is the best suited for your sales team given their current phase, there are steps to take to ensure the introduction of the technology is effective.

I was working with a small sales team of six employees, and during our time together, questions continued to arise about how to use the CRM software. Specifically, there were differing opinions on when to enter a lead into the software and what triggered transitioning a lead from one pipeline stage to the next.

The result of these differing views on when and how to move a prospect through the sales pipeline was that information wasn't accurate. As a result, the pipeline seemed far less robust than it was, so the sales leader was consistently on the team to boost their performance.

Some examples of the common issues the team faced because of this misalignment and confusion included the following:

- The number of leads generated was far less than expected.
- The opportunities captured didn't reflect reality.
- Forecasts of sales were inaccurate, resulting in the manager micromanaging the team.
- Team members complained of the distrust demonstrated by the sales manager.

This is what I refer to as a circular issue. The employees feared entering information into the CRM to protect themselves if they were too optimistic about opportunities, resulting in the sales leader believing that the team was underperforming. As he pushed for better results, the team pulled back even further in their efforts to add to and update the CRM.

My experience with technology, as you may have figured out by now, is that the devil is in the details. I'm not suggesting you spend excessive time analyzing software options for your sales team, but you should engage your team in your assessment. Recognize that choosing the wrong software can completely derail your efforts to build an unstoppable sales team. But on the other hand, selecting and implementing the right software can accelerate your ability to create a robust, high-performing, unstoppable team.

| Steps to Introduce Technology into a Sales Team |
| --- |
| 1. Capture Existing Sales Processes. |
| 2. Identify Existing Software and Technology in Use. |
| 3. Agree upon Gaps, Weaknesses, and Blind Spots. |
| 4. Identify Software or Technology to Address Gaps. |
| 5. Assess Potential Impacts of Technology or Software. |
| 6. Select Technology or Software to Review. |
| 7. Have the Sales Team Assess Functionality. |
| 8. Speak to Existing Users of Selected Tech or Software. |
| 9. Select the Best Tech or Software Option. |
| 10. Measure Improvements Against Expectations. |

**FIGURE 12.2**
Steps to introduce technology into your sales team.

We need to come from a position of recognizing that your sales team already has a proven sales process, so any software they adopt must equate to improved results such as reduced labor intensity, increased efficiency, etc. If the results include significant changes to how the sales team operates and it doesn't improve efficiency, then it is possible technology isn't necessary.

Many software providers will try to convince you that their software represents industry best practices (and they'll strongly encourage you to follow best practices). But, in the words of Public Enemy,[49] "Don't Believe the Hype!" In many instances, "best practices" simply means the platform has been built to serve many different types of companies or industries.

Let's look at the process I use with clients to assess and introduce technology that aids their sales teams' performance. Figure 12.2 depicts the steps which we'll describe below.

## SHAWN'S TECHNOLOGY INTRODUCTION PROCESS

1. Capture Your Existing Sales Process(es)
   Document your existing sales process steps, allowing you to identify the impacts of any new software or technology, good or bad. This step is also important as many software providers build their

products to sell to various industries, satisfying as many different users as possible. Selecting the wrong software while not recognizing the impact on your sales process can be a nightmare!

2. Identify Your Existing Software and Technology in Use
Before looking at any new technology or software, consider the existing software you have today and ensure you recognize the full functionality and features. You'll be surprised at the additional features or options you can introduce that will improve your sales process without any additional cost or that require the adoption of new technology.

3. Agree Upon Any Gaps, Weaknesses, or Blind Spots with Your Existing Sales Process
Before identifying any area of your sales process to introduce technology, ensure you involve your sales team. Additionally, you may learn that the technology or software you are considering will have minimal impact on improving efficiency, quality, or productivity.

4. Identify Technology or Software that can Improve the Sales Process
There are several, if not dozens, of competitors for every new piece of software or technology. Take your time with the first solution you come across. If, for example, you are considering new software to assist in finding leads, although I've given you one option above, there are dozens of similar options, all with their pros and cons. Understand your options before you make any decisions.

5. Assess the Impacts of the New Technology or Software
Once you have narrowed down some software or new tech options, look closely at the impacts on people and processes. Again, I recommend using two columns on a sheet (i.e., drawbacks versus opportunities). Next, you involve members of your sales team who have been part of the assessment thus far and have developed their views and opinions of the options they've witnessed.

6. Select Tech or Software Options to Review
With a clear understanding of the software or technology available to you, take the time to select one or two options to review and test. Examples include watching a demonstration, using a test site, or having some team members try out the software for some time, reporting on their findings. Whatever the case, do not jump to negotiating or purchasing without having your team first test the software and set up criteria for measurement before step #7 below.

7. Have Your Sales Team Assess the Functionality of the new Software
   Involve your team in testing the software or technology's features, functionality, and impact on their ability to sell. Provide questions before testing and ensure you receive feedback, not the least of which should include how it integrates, the benefits and features most used, and any bugs or issues caused in navigating the existing sales process, etc.

8. Speak to Existing Users of the New Tech or Software as Part of Your Assessment
   As your sales team is testing the new software or technology, ask the vendor to share with you some references with whom you can speak. In addition, you want to connect with other end users and ask them questions arising from your observations and the team's experiences as they test or trial the new software. Warning: if the vendor is unwilling or unable to connect you with other users, I will walk away from their technology, as this can be a warning sign that their other users are not as happy as they might suggest.

9. Select the Best Option
   With a clear understanding of the drawbacks versus opportunities, the next step is selecting your ideal software or technology. Although the selection will be as a team, this is likely something you'll have to lead as someone who controls your P&L or have budget responsibility. Hint: if you have a fixed budget to invest that is less than the asking price, try negotiating at the end of the month or the end of the year for possible discount opportunities.

10. Measure Improvements Against Expectations Using Observations and Feedback
    Once you've selected your new software or technology and have gone through training, make sure to set and periodically revisit the benefits you had expected to achieve. Unfortunately, many sales leaders fail at this point. They never return to ask, "did we achieve what we expected?" Once you revisit expectations and find that the answer is "no," see the bonus tip below!
    **Bonus Tip:** You Can Always Revert to Old Methods!

If you find the technology you've introduced is not working as you expect and it's creating more setbacks or a reduction in productivity or sales rather than improvements, you can go back to how you used to do things.

You can! Not being willing to do this is simply a sign of ego and demonstrates to your team that your desire to look good is more important than their ability to sell efficiently and effectively. There are other ingredients for building an unstoppable sales team!

With technology selected that will aid, rather than hinder, the performance of your sales team, and the team involved in the process, you're well on your way to a high-performing sales team that will be unstoppable!

### UNSTOPPABLE SALES TEAM ACTION STEPS:

1. What software or technology are you using today?
2. Is it as effective as it could be (ask your sales team for feedback)?
3. Where might new software or technology further accelerate your sales team's performance?
4. How can you prioritize introducing any new technology or software to gain the most impact for your team?

For a copy of my Sales Technology Selection checklist, see www.unstop pablesales.team

Let's continue our discussion on methods to accelerate your sales team's performance to unstoppable levels in Chapter 13!

# 13

## *Accelerating Your Unstoppable Sales Team's Performance*

Just remember, once you are over the hill you will begin to pick up speed.

**Arthur Schopenhauer**
*German Philosopher*

By this point you've worked hard to build your unstoppable sales team, painstakingly following the steps we've covered throughout this book, so now what? Well, if you're like most of my clients, your goal is to continuously accelerate the performance and results of your sales team, so you're always searching for *what's next*.

With your unstoppable sales team now built and in action, there are some critical areas for you to focus on in the near term if you want to further accelerate the results of your team's performance. These include skills development, process improvement, and accountability in applying the concepts discussed in this book.

Let's start with the area that can have the most significant overall impact on your sale teams performance, skills development.

## ADVANCING YOUR TEAM'S SALES SKILLS

Much of my sales teamwork focuses on introducing and applying advanced selling skills. I've learned that although continuously learning sales skills is essential to success, so is taking the time to apply those

**FIGURE 13.1**
Sales negotiation method.

skills. In other words, you need to practice and apply the fundamentals to gain the experience necessary to find value and the opportunity to use more advanced skills.

Let's look at an example.

Fundamentally, negotiation is considered a step in the sales process, which often occurs after a proposal or quote is issued and before it closes. As a result, negotiations are something your sales team practices while addressing objections and attempting to close a deal.

Advanced selling requires you consider negotiations not as a stage in the sales process but as the process itself. From your first conversation with a prospect until you close the deal, you are negotiating what I call YATNA or Your Alternative to a Negotiated Agreement. Figure 13.1 outlines the steps to this advanced approach to negotiations.

Negotiations then is an essential element of your sales process and is one of five main areas to consider as advanced selling skills for your sales team. The five areas are as follows:

1. **Advanced prospecting skills:** Top sales professionals practice what I refer to as the ABP's (Always Be Prospecting) of sales. Helping sales professionals and teams recognize the need to consistently apply different methods to prospecting and to ensure they prospect continuously.

2. **Advanced negotiation skills:** As shared in the earlier example, high-performing sales professionals recognize negotiations are not a stage in their sales process but that it begins at the initial point of contact with their prospect and continues throughout the buyer relationship.

3. **Advanced discovery narratives:** Most sales professionals become accustomed to asking surface questions such as "What are your pain points?" or "What would you like to improve about your current product/service?" These questions are suitable for new sales professionals, helping them to get comfortable with asking questions of their prospect; however, they will not lead to being a high-performing sales professional. In advanced discovery narratives, I share with sales teams how to uncover key prospect objectives, solicit input from outside referral sources, and guide the conversation using questions.

4. **Power language for influence:** One of the most underrated yet powerful tools a sales professional has is their language. Language determines the level of trust a prospect has in the sales professional, so choosing the correct language at the right time is critical to success. Examples include emotion-invoking words and phrases and using language to build unbreakable rapport and trust.

5. **Advanced closing skills:** The most common challenge I present to any more advanced sales professionals I work with is speeding up their closing. Many successful sales professionals cling to their processes rather than remain confident in their skills. Accelerating the pace of the sales process and speeding to the close is a skill that can be developed and applied, enabling more sales (and more revenue) for each sales professional.

There are other areas to consider; however, in my experience, focusing on any (or all) of the skills above will dramatically accelerate your unstoppable sales team's success and results.

Next to instantiating the use of advanced sales skills for your team, the next most important area to consider to improve your sales team's performance is to improve your performance as a sales leader.

## ADVANCING YOUR LEADERSHIP SKILLS

Building and leading an unstoppable sales team is no easy feat (that's why teams that perform at this level aren't that common!). It takes persistence, patience, focus, creativity, and dedication on your part to make

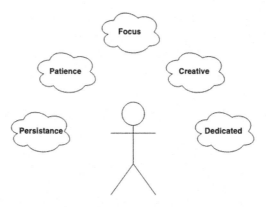

**Unstoppable Sales Leader Priorities**

**FIGURE 13.2**
Priorities for building an unstoppable sales team.

consistent and meaningful progress. Figure 13.2 presents how these work in unison.

1. You must be persistent in your pursuit. There will be barriers, push-back, and other priorities that will present themselves. Regardless, you must remain constant in your approach, methods, and behaviors to ensure your team recognizes your commitment to their success.
2. Your patience will be tested. There will be times when new methods or approaches take longer to realize than you expect. Be patient, the strategies I've shared in this book are in use by hundreds of sales leaders with tremendous success, but it does take time.
3. You will need to remain focused on your end goal. Keep your priorities and issues focused on what matters: the consistent pursuit of developing and advancing your sales team's performance. Remember, their success is your success.
4. There will be times when you need to be creative. There may be software your team wants to introduce; however, you don't have a budget to support it; or there may be new ideas you bring to the team that they don't like. You'll need to be creative to introduce new methods, processes, and software when the environment or circumstances could be more optimal.

5. You must remain dedicated to the success of your team. Like first impressions, it only takes one misstatement or inappropriate behavior to show your team that their success isn't significant. Dedicate yourself and your role to supporting your team in achieving success.

Placing focus on and continuously practicing these five priorities will ensure that you'll remain on track despite setbacks, resorting back to old leadership habits, or any frustration with the speed at which your team transitions. Remember, building your sales team is a marathon, not a sprint.

Suppose you do find yourself challenged to break old leadership habits or you are seeking additional guidance. In that case, you should engage a good coach who has experience in building and leading an unstoppable sales team. Someone who can help you navigate the challenges and obstacles that will consistently present themselves along the journey. Most high-performing athletes have coaches to continually push them to improve their skills, as do many CEOs and political leaders. Maybe it's time you consider the same?

In some instances, having a good coach who fits your style and who can assist you in achieving your objectives (such as building your unstoppable sales team) can be a simple yet effective method of accelerating the development of your team.

In the coaching work I do with sales executives and leaders across North America in building their own unstoppable sales teams, I've found several ways a good coach can support your journey.

---

## HOW A GOOD COACH CAN HELP BUILD YOUR UNSTOPPABLE SALES TEAM

1. **Develop your unstoppable sales team plan:** Every sales leader is in a different circumstance when building their sales team. You may be in the early phases of building your team from the ground up, and a coach can assist you in identifying the shortest path to successfully building your team.
2. **Rebuild your sales team:** In some situations, you may have a mature sales team and want to rebuild the team to increase its

performance. In this instance, a good coach can help you quickly identify what changes to make within your team, including the group members, and how to prioritize the most critical to your success.

3. **Improve the individual performance of members on your team:** Sometimes, you may face challenges in improving your team members' performance. A good coach who has worked with hundreds of sales professionals can help you identify the shortest path to improving performance. Additionally, a coach can ensure you don't waste time trying to improve the performance of someone who isn't a good fit for the team.

4. **Launch of a new product or entering a new market:** Equipping and motivating a sales team to launch a new product or enter a new market can be a challenge, particularly if the sales leader doesn't have experience. In this instance, a good sales coach can guide the sales leader to take the steps necessary to shorten the time needed to transition from launch to achieving the desired market share.

5. **Access to best practices:** In some cases, I've found my coaching clients seek access to best practices, enabling them to short-cut the time it takes to accelerate their sales team's performance. Working with a credible coach who has access to and can introduce proven best practices is an excellent way to shorten the path to building an unstoppable sales team.

There are other reasons why you may want a coach. Some of my best clients have told me that having me as their coach or advisor is like an insurance policy, helping them progress faster than they could have and avoiding costly mistakes. Whatever your reason, and whomever you choose, consider a coach as a key tool to building and advancing your unstoppable sales team.

Whether it's using a coach, introducing new technology, changing your sales processes, or making adjustments in how your sales team operates to meet the ever-changing needs of today's busy buyers, there will be consistent changes impacting your sales team. However, HOW you introduce these changes will determine their degree of success. For example, I've seen a new sales processes for lead capture add a minimum of 2 hours of data entry for a team of sales professionals offering no clear benefits over the previous information collected.

As you might imagine, there are right and wrong ways to introduce change to ensure it supports the continued acceleration of your sales team's performance. To ensure your success, let's discuss the right way.

## THE BIG SHORT: THE COUNTERINTUITIVE WAY TO INTRODUCE CHANGES TO YOUR TEAM

In the movie the Big Short,[50] Michael Burry, played by Christian Bale, uncovers a housing bubble that he expects will lead to a market crash in 2007. His realization prompts him to approach well-known financial institutions and propose creating a credit default swap market, which would allow him to bet against (short) market-based mortgage back securities, with the expectation of making a significant profit. Before this time, no one had ever bet against mortgage-backed securities, leading Burry to stand out as someone likely to lose. Unfortunately, his hunch was correct.

Before you roll your eyes and begin thinking this is going to be some boring section discussing change management, hold up! There is a specific approach you'll need to take if you want your sales team to accept and adopt a change to their already proven (or comfortable) methods. Figure 13.3 outlines this approach.

| Introducing Change in Your Sales Team | | | | |
|---------|----------|-------|----------|--------|
| ASSESS | CONTRAST | PILOT | BENEFITS | LAUNCH |
| | | | | |
| | | Stages to Introduce Change ⟹ | | |
| | | | | |

**FIGURE 13.3**
Introducing changes to your unstoppable sales team.

## SHAWN'S STEPS FOR INTRODUCING CHANGE TO YOUR SALES TEAM

### Step 1

The first step is to ASSESS the change's impact on your current sales methods and processes. Evaluating impact is achieved by asking the following questions:

1. What are the perceived benefits of this change?
2. What existing procedures or practices will be impacted?
3. What will be the impact on our sales team's productivity?
4. How much more effective will our sales team be as a result?

### Step 2

The second step is to CONTRAST the change.

1. What additional effort or actions will be required of the sales team?
2. What benefits will be realized for the sales team?
3. What benefits will be recognized for the broader organization?
4. Will this change improve our competitive position?

### Step 3

If the change is perceived as beneficial at this point, you'll want to PILOT the approach among your sales team using the following:

1. What is the best method to test this change and contrast it against our theories above?
2. How can we monitor the change to confirm its effectiveness?
3. With whom will we share the pilot results?
4. How often will we assess progress?

## Step 4

Once the pilot has been completed, you will need to decide whether to proceed with the change. The degree to which you realize the expected BENEFITS compared to the level of effort and perceived impacts will be your deciding factors.

1. What benefits did we realize from the pilot?
2. What effort was required and how did this impact productivity and effectiveness?
3. Do the benefits outweigh these efforts?
4. Should we proceed with introducing the change because of the above?

## Step 5

Once you've decided if you will proceed, the next step is to LAUNCH your change fully. Use the following to guide you in these efforts:

1. Where should we begin with introducing this change?
2. Should the change be introduced fully or just partially?
3. How will we provide the necessary training and education on the difference?
4. Who will be involved? How will we best involve them?

There will always be new technology, new ideas, and new methods to introduce that you'll expect will improve your sales team's performance. When this happens, don't fall prey to shiny object syndrome. Instead, follow the simple process above to ensure your team will benefit from the change and confirm the impact the change will have on your team's ability to perform at the highest levels.

Using this approach, you'll engage your sales team in determining when and how to introduce change, ensuring they are readily adopted and accepted (and they won't resent you for the change!). As you might imagine, this goes a long way toward *retaining your sales team*. But what if you need to introduce additional team members to your sales team? There is a process for this that I call Sales Performer Attraction.

## ATTRACTING SALES TALENT WITH SALES PERFORMER ATTRACTION

We've discussed in previous chapters the best methods to hire and retain your unstoppable sales team. However, keeping everyone in today's job market will take much work. For this reason, sales leaders should always look for new talent for their team, even if it doesn't seem like they'll need them. The approach I recommend is the Sales Performer Attraction Method, which is an ongoing process that attracts talent to you rather than the other way around.

While leading a team of 10 salespeople early in my career, I had the uncomfortable challenge of having one resign to pursue a new business venture at the same time as I was redeploying another to a new role better suited for their skills. It's not tricky covering off one vacant territory while you seek new candidates, but two at a time, considering the size of each rep's part, took a lot of work.

I decided that never again would I be faced with the challenge of searching for, recruiting, and hiring new sales talent. It was then that I first came up with what I refer to as the Sales Performer Attraction method which ensured I never had to recruit again. My clients who have used this method have had similar results, so it's something you should strongly consider if you want to avoid the time and energy required to recruit and hire new sales talent (Figure 13.4).

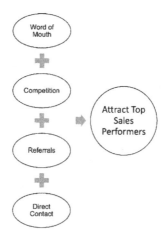

**FIGURE 13.4**
Sales performer attraction.

The method works as follows:

**Word of mouth:** As a strong sales leader, you should always be discussing your sales team (the culture, comradery, and opportunities) publicly. Share highlights while networking, mention tidbits in public presentations, share pictures of the team on social media, etc. The goal is to create word-of-mouth buzz about how great your sales team is and how well they are doing. When you do so, you'll generate word-of-mouth buzz about the benefits of your team, which will, in turn, attract outsiders to inquire about opportunities to join.

**Competition:** When your team learns of and shares information about other sales reps with the competition, make sure you reach out to connect on some level (assuming they are any good). My favorite approach is to click on LinkedIn with a message saying, "Always looking to connect with other like-minded sales professionals." When you connect with the competition, you open doors for potential candidates to approach you when they become tired or frustrated with their current employer.

**Suppliers:** Sales representatives from your suppliers visit your company regularly. Have you ever taken the time to meet and learn more about them? These can be a great source of new talent to tap into, and you can know more about how they work by speaking with your internal departments, such as procurement or operations.

**Referrals:** Let it be known to your sales team that any sales talent they refer in and who you decided to hire is worth something. Make the benefits something they will appreciate, including a cash incentive, vacation time, dinner with the CEO, etc. I've known companies who have built their unstoppable sales team with this one strategy alone, never having posted or pursued any sales talent!

**Direct contact:** As a sales professional, you always run into sales talent at trade shows, events, and even sales training. Be sure to seek talent before a team member leaves or when you have a new vacancy. This reactive approach can lead to selecting the "best candidate," given your options. Instead, spend time making direct contact with anyone in sales which you meet that catches your eye. Build this network and stay in touch so that you have a stable sales talent to reach out to when an opportunity arises.

## THE FUTURE OF SALES TALENT (AND WHY YOU NEED TO BUILD AN UNSTOPPABLE SALES TEAM)

I don't own a crystal ball, but if I did, there would be a few tips I'd leave you with that will help you in your journey to build and sustain your unstoppable sales team.

The demands of sales talent are evolving. Free time and the ability to work remotely while having greater control over how one works is increasingly important to sales professionals. Shift with the times, listen to your team's requests, and ensure you adjust to meet their needs.

Technology will continue to influence how we sell. As the demographic of our sales teams shift (those entering the sales profession are getting younger)), so to are our buyers' demographics. So be prepared to introduce technology that your team wants to try but be sure to use the strategies laid out in Chapter 12 on how you select and integrate that technology.

There will be less talent available. Sales was once a career that those who were social and didn't fit elsewhere landed. Although this wasn't the case for everyone, a large percentage of people in sales were "in transition" in their careers. Some just never made it back out. Today fewer younger generations are "transitioning," and as a result, the available talent is less and less. Work hard to hold onto your sales talent and practice the Sales Performer Attraction method above, and you'll always be flush with leads in the new talent market when available talent is shrinking.

Lastly, and most importantly, it would be best if you changed the times. Your style and approach to leading your team must change as your team changes. Attempting to apply leadership strategies that were effective 10 years ago will result in your sales team believing that you need to be in touch. Instead, study new leadership techniques and use them. Continuously improve your emotional intelligence and spend time uncovering how your sales team prefers to operate so that you can remain proactive in supporting their journey.

I'll leave you with this. When my father retired around 60, I was still leading sales teams. One day, frustrated with my team, I was telling him how I looked forward to the day I could retire and not have to deal with all the issues and challenges brought forth by my team. He grinned and said, Shawn, when I look back on my career, regardless of how challenging leading a team is, it's that impact I have on the team that are the memories I cherish most.

Remember this. You are impacting the lives of your sales team, both directly and indirectly. There will be days that you are frustrated, but know that you are having an impact, and the memories you carry will be of the impact you made.

For your Unstoppable Sales Team Action Planner, see www.unstoppa blesales.team

# Closing the Deal

My purpose in writing this book is to provide you with a framework to build strength in your sales team, and renewed enthusiasm in your chosen career as a sales leader.

My mission in life is to help sales executives and leaders like you create an environment of Unstoppable Sales$^{SM}$, so if you are eager for even more strategies to accelerate your sales team, make sure to visit my website at www.shawncasemore.com.

There you'll find helpful tips and strategies designed to support you on your sales leadership journey, shared in various formats including video, audio, and print form.

Remember, the most important component in building your unstoppable sales team is you, and you aren't alone in your journey.

# Endnotes

1. https://www.thedailymeal.com/eat/taste-test-definitive-ranking-12-cheerios-flavors
2. https://www.gartner.ca/en/sales/insights/b2b-buying-journey
3. https://www.trustradius.com/vendor-blog/2022-b2b-buying-disconnect-the-age-of-the-self-serve-buyer
4. https://en.wikipedia.org/wiki/Locus_of_control
5. https://elearningindustry.com/the-adult-learning-theory-andragogy-of-malcolm-knowles
6. https://discinsights.com/william-marston
7. https://www.britannica.com/biography/Mia-Hamm
8. https://en.wikipedia.org/wiki/Talladega_Nights:_The_Ballad_of_Ricky_Bobby
9. https://en.wikipedia.org/wiki/Expectancy_theory
10. https://en.wikipedia.org/wiki/Victor_Vroom
11. https://shawncasemore.com/books/the-unstoppable-organization/
12. https://en.wikipedia.org/wiki/Peyton_Manning
13. https://en.wikipedia.org/wiki/Albert_Einstein
14. https://en.wikipedia.org/wiki/Pontiac_Sunfire
15. https://www.britannica.com/topic/creativity
16. https://www.goodreads.com/book/show/40745.Mindset
17. https://hbr.org/2012/04/the-new-science-of-building-great-teams
18. https://www.amazon.com/Mindset-Psychology-Carol-S-Dweck/dp/0345472322
19. https://en.wikipedia.org/wiki/Frederick_Herzberg
20. https://en.wikipedia.org/wiki/Frederick_Winslow_Taylor
21. https://en.wikipedia.org/wiki/Maslow%27s_hierarchy_of_needs
22. https://en.wikipedia.org/wiki/Richard_Branson
23. https://en.wikipedia.org/wiki/William_Moulton_Marston
24. https://en.wikipedia.org/wiki/Carl_Jung
25. https://alanweiss.com/
26. https://en.wikipedia.org/wiki/John_Whitmore_(racing_driver)
27. http://www.thesolutionsfocus.com/
28. https://en.wikipedia.org/wiki/Maslow%27s_hierarchy_of_needs
29. https://en.wikipedia.org/wiki/William_Moulton_Marston
30. https://www.coxautoinc.com/market-insights/2019-dealership-staffing-study-released/
31. https://www.zoominfo.com/
32. https://bombbomb.com/
33. https://www.activecampaign.com/
34. https://www.tidio.com/
35. https://www.copilotai.com/
36. https://www.salesforce.com/ca/
37. https://spotio.com/
38. https://www.dropbox.com/home

39. https://www.pandadoc.com/
40. https://zoom.us/
41. https://www.apple.com/ca/keynote/
42. https://www.surveymonkey.com/
43. https://www.whatsapp.com/
44. https://circle.so/
45. https://trello.com/en
46. https://www.hoopla.net/
47. https://www.brainshark.com/
48. https://www.outreach.io/
49. https://en.wikipedia.org/wiki/Public_Enemy
50. https://en.wikipedia.org/wiki/The_Big_Short_(film)

# Index

Note: Locators in *italics* represent figures in the text.

Printed in the United States
by Baker & Taylor Publisher Services